More
Great Good
Dairy-free
Desserts
Naturally

Sin-sational Sumptuous Treats

Fran Costigan

Book Publishing Company
Summertown, Tennessee

Cover design: Warren Jefferson
Cover & interior photos: Warren Jefferson
Back cover author photo: Dan Demetriad
Interior design: Gwynelle Dismukes

Published in the United States by

Book Publishing Company
P.O. Box 99
Summertown, TN 38483
1-888-260-8458

Printed in the United States

ISBN-13 978-1-57067-183-8
ISBN-10 1-57067-183-4

15 14 13 12 11 10 09 08 07 06   1 2 3 4 5 6 7 8 9

Costigan, Fran.
  More great good dairy-free desserts naturally : sin-sational sumptuous treats / Fran Costigan.
     p. cm.
Includes bibliographical references and index.
ISBN-13: 978-1-57067-183-8
ISBN-10: 1-57067-183-4
 1. Desserts. 2. Cookery (Natural foods) I. Title.

TX773.C6345 2006
641.8'6--dc22

2005034108

Featured on the cover:
Colossal Chocolate Cake,
page 150

This book is dedicated to Tracy, Michael, Linda, and Georgia Lili
my most favorite sweets.

Contents

Acknowledgments

More Great Good Desserts Naturally involved the hard work and support of many people.

I am grateful to Annemarie Colbin, author and founding director of the Natural Gourmet Institute for Health and Culinary Arts, for sparking my interest in natural foods. I know I can always count on Annemarie for up-to-date, practical answers to my questions. Thank you to Jenny Matthau, the director, and the entire staff at the Natural Gourmet Institute for Health and Culinary Arts, for supporting my classes. I thank Rick Smilow, president of the Institute of Culinary Education, for inviting me to add my vegan desserts classes to the vast array of courses offered, and to the staff that has worked to make my classes successful.

I want to thank everyone at Book Publishing Company, Warren, Barb B., Barbara J., Gwynelle, Anna, and Bob, for their support, and for being honestly nice people. Cynthia Holzapfel, my editor, deserves a medal for her patience, good humor, and encouragement. I wish to thank Jo Stepaniak, who worked with me during the early days of this project and offered such good insight and information.

I have the very good luck to count among my friends and mentors many talented chefs and cookbook authors who have freely shared information and more: Ken Bergeron, Chad Sarno, Joy Pierson and Bart Potenza, Cathy DiCocco, Kevin Dunn, Bill Telepan, Jeanette Maier, Ann Cooper, Shirley King, Dana Jacobi, Linda Baker, and Linda Long. For encouragement, support, and practical advice, I want to say thank you to my long-distance colleagues and friends, the well-published cookbook author Bryanna Clark

Grogan, from Canada, and Mimi Clark, owner of VegGourmet Cooking School, in Fairfax, Virginia, both of whom shared their considerable knowledge generously and answered email queries quickly. And big thanks and hugs to my friends at the North American Vegetarian Society (NAVS) and EarthSave for their good works, great conferences, and loads of fun.

Thank you, Leah Breier, for always making time to answer a question. Cousin Sheila, your books inspire me and our talks nourish me.

Without the men and women behind the genius bar at the Apple Store in Soho who found lost files and calmed me when my iBook crashed, this book would not have gone from computer to the printed page. I am sure I visited every single genius, but Francis George, who went beyond what seemed possible, and Cliff, the calm vegan techie, you are among the kindest folks I know.

I am very grateful to Kevin Takasato, who did his graduate internship with me and was always on time, kept meticulous notes of the recipes he so carefully tested, and was delightfully enthusiastic about his favorites, and to Sarah McFarlane, my assistant, who hit the floor running and got everything finished on time. Thank you, Katherine Raymond, for your sharp eyes and good questions, and to my friends and neighbors who gladly ate the cakes and cookies, puddings, and whatever else I was testing, and offered great feedback.

Tracy, Michael, and Linda, you light up my life. I thank you for your encouragement and good ideas.

Finally, I am deeply appreciative of my students, whose enthusiasm and good ideas inspired me to write this book and make my work an ongoing delight.

Introduction

I eat sweets every day, with pleasure, not guilt—and in moderation, as part of a diet based on whole organic foods. This was not always the case.

I was born into a family obsessed with both sweets and dieting, so it may have been inevitable that I would get caught up in the exhausting cycle of eating too many cookies, too much cake, ice cream, and chocolate, then none at all. Deprivation led to my overeating sweets again, and so it went. I think I intuitively knew that a piece of chocolate couldn't really be an enemy to be resisted with resolve, but it was years before I took steps that led to understanding and making peace with my cravings.

My grandmother was a wonderful, cheerful cook and baker, and I spent a lot of time in her kitchen. I was fascinated with all aspects of food and meal preparation. The frequent dinner parties I liked to give ended with multicourse desserts, and I often volunteered to make desserts for local fund-raising events.

I decided to enroll in the New York Restaurant School while my two children were in primary school, wondering if a career in the culinary field might be possible. It was an exciting time for me, and although I enjoyed the entire curriculum, it was the dessert classes that held the most appeal. I was excited after graduation to begin working as the baker in a gourmet take-out food shop on Manhattan's Upper East Side. Eagerly, I started early in the morning to bake muffins, scones, popovers, cookies, pies, and cakes. My desserts were popular, and I enjoyed the work, but my energy, which fluctuated wildly, was often very low. I had to nap every day after work and too often was moody and cranky. In fact, I left my job after only six months, feeling I did not have the stamina to do the work I liked so much.

During that time, I heard about the Food and Healing course taught by the founder of the Natural Gourmet Cookery School, Annemarie Colbin, and bought the book of the same name. I found the data linking food and health fascinating and wanted to learn more, so I enrolled. Annemarie teaches that no one specific diet is ideal for everyone, because we are individuals, but there is one diet that is bad for us all—the SAD (standard American diet). Bingo! I knew it was my breakfasts of a piece of some dessert left from the day before and big lattes, the cookie breaks before lunch, and so on throughout the day and evening that had led to my fatigue, moodiness, and not feeling well. As I read more of the compelling evidence linking food and health, I wondered if the stomachaches and allergies I had suffered since childhood would be alleviated if I eliminated dairy, eggs, and white sugar from my diet. I was astonished and thrilled when this was precisely the case. I felt terrific. I woke rested, my energy was high and even, and unfortunately, I became a member of the food police. No desserts for me or for you, I told my family and friends, and anyone else I managed to lecture. I resolved never to make desserts again. Even though I was not experiencing out-of-control cravings, I missed my sweet treats—and putting birthday candles into a baked apple was less than satisfying.

I noticed that folks like me who shunned all sweets were glancing with longing at the jugs of maple syrup in the classroom. I began to consider the idea of balance. I wondered if it was possible to make excellent versions of traditional desserts using only wholesome, healthful ingredients without dairy, eggs, and white sugar. I had to learn about the properties of whole grain flours, sweeteners, and other natural ingredients. After many misses, I found that when I married foundation technique with natural ingredients, I was able to develop some excellent recipes. Vanilla, chocolate, and lemon cakes were first, followed by all categories of desserts.

My first collection of recipes was published as *Great Good Desserts Naturally* in 1999 and has been reprinted five times, I am happy to say. The best part for me has been hearing from new and experienced bakers all around the world who tell me they are happy to finally have an alternative way to make and enjoy their favorite desserts.

Recently, with my notebooks bulging with exceptional recipes gleaned from years of teaching at the Natural Gourmet Cookery School and the Institute of Culinary Education, working as a consultant in professional kitchens, and baking custom special-occasion cakes for private clients, I agreed that it was time to write a new, more comprehensive book of nondairy and egg-free desserts. I am confident that as you make the recipes, you will know without a doubt that you can have your cake and eat it too. Now let's go into the kitchen and make something good.

Chapter 1 . . . Getting Started

Introducing More Great Good Desserts Naturally

Eat your fruits and vegetables but make sure you leave room for dessert, as long as the dessert tastes excellent and is made with healthful, honest ingredients, that is. Serve it proudly and enjoy. This is the secret to having your cake and eating it too.

More and more people have noticed the huge role food plays in the way they feel physically and emotionally, in their conversations and in their social lives. Many of my students and dessert clients (or someone in their family) are in the process of eliminating or have already eliminated dairy, eggs, and white sugar from their diets. Sometimes the change is a result of advice from a medical practitioner: lower your cholesterol and intake of saturated fat. Others learn they are allergic to eggs or are lactose intolerant (studies indicate that we are all lactose intolerant to some degree). For

still others, the decision is made based on compassion for animals (vegans), or religious beliefs, such as Seventh Day Adventists and those following a kosher diet.

You may have reduced or eliminated all animal foods because you find the evidence linking milk and other dairy products, refined sugar, saturated fats, artificial ingredients, and additive-laden foods to health problems too compelling to ignore. The reasons are not mutually exclusive, but whatever led to the choice, virtually no one wants to give up desserts. Perhaps when the change in diet is new, some people may think, as I did, that all sweet foods are verboten, but this conviction rarely lasts or works; few of us want to give up desserts entirely. Eating a satisfying dessert makes people feel happy—desserts are celebratory. Even those who scrutinize each gram of fat or shun every kind of sweet talk wistfully about their favorite birthday cake, holiday pie, or childhood snack.

For several years now I have been teaching "my kind" of pastry classes to an ever more diverse group of people. Some are just curious (How can you make real cakes without milk and eggs?), in transition, or already dairy- and egg-free. Many parents take a class to learn how to make a birthday cake for their lactose intolerant or egg-allergic child, and of course, want the cake to taste good enough for school friends accustomed to eating mainstream cakes. I began to realize just how widespread this issue was as professional chefs and students in culinary school showed up in my classes. When a classically trained French pastry chef took a class, confiding that his young son could no longer eat dairy or eggs and that he needed to learn to bake differently, I knew the days of having to defend "my type" of baking were over.

I decided it was time to write a new, more comprehensive dessert cookbook to address the need I saw (and the requests I got) for recipes that could be made with more accessible, less expensive ingredients (light natural cane sugar in place of maple syrup, for example). But I would continue to honor the promise I made to myself when I left the "butter-cream-sugar" pastry kitchen for the "nondairy, egg-free, no white sugar" pastry kitchen of the '80s and use only substitutes that were real foods and minimally processed. Desserts made with my recipes will taste and look as good, if not better, than their traditional counterparts.

This book has been designed as a complete course in nondairy, egg-free baking, but you can go directly to any recipe, in any order you wish; each one is detailed and complete. The first recipe chapter, Gels, Creams, Puddings, and Sauces, teaches you how to use plant-based gelling agents and powdered starch, two foundation ingredients necessary to nondairy and egg-free baking. The next chapter, Cookies, Bars, and Little Bites, introduces flours and leavening agents and provides instruction in the proper techniques for measuring and mixing simple batters. In Chapter 4, you will practice making batters for cobblers, crisps, biscuits, muffins, and more. Chapter 5 is all about cakes, from plain to elaborate, while Chapter 6, Pies and Tarts, gives you the tools to master pastry dough. The recipes in the final chapter range from baked apples to smoothies, granola, sorbets, and candies.

Organic Makes Sense

If you incorporate organic foods into your diet, your food will taste better, you will feel better, and small farmers will benefit—so will our planet. The term "organic" refers to the way agricultural products are grown and processed. On organic farms soil fertility is maintained and replenished without the use of toxic and persistent pesticides and fertilizers. Organic foods are minimally processed without artificial ingredients, preservatives, or irradiation to maintain the integrity of the food. The more organic food you purchase, the more big businesses will notice and the more the price for organic food will come tumbling down. Vote with your fork.

Essential Ingredients

Today the nondairy and egg-free baker has many options, as natural and organic ingredients have entered the mainstream. Cartons of soymilk as well as soy creamer stand next to dairy milk and cream in supermarkets. Tofu comes in many varieties. There is a dizzying, if not confusing, array of granulated natural sweeteners; in fact, the Domino sugar company is now selling organic sugar. I have organic molasses and organic cornstarch in my pantry, two products I would not use in a nonorganic form. A wide variety of excellent organic and fair trade chocolates and cocoa powders are offered (see page 22 for more information on fair trade chocolate).

I've heard many people say that they want to make and eat more healthful foods, but are not willing to change every ingredient in their pantry at once. This is understandable. I believe making informed choices over time and doing the best you can do is the way to go. All the ingredients needed to make the recipes in this book are available in most markets; if you can't find them in your area, consult the companies listed on page 210.

Essential Ingredients and Equipment for the Nondairy, Egg-Free Baker's Dessert Kitchen

Everything needed to make all the recipes in the book is listed here. Purchase what you need for basic baking and add to your pantry as you wish.

Sweeteners, granulated:

Cane sugar, dark whole (Sucanat and Rapadura are two popular brands, but there are many others, and bulk is available)

Cane sugar, light natural (Florida Crystals is a popular brand, but there are many others and bulk is available.)

Maple sugar

Sweeteners, liquid:

Barley malt

Brown rice syrup

Maple syrup, pure, Grade A dark amber (not pancake syrup which is made with refined sweeteners and maple flavor)

Molasses, organic

Liquids and moist ingredients:

Apple cider vinegar

Applesauce, unsweetened

Canola oil, expeller-pressed organic

Coconut milk, unsweetened, full fat

Extracts:
  Almond
  Coconut
  Lemon
  Orange
  Vanilla, pure (not imitation vanillin)

Fruit juices, apple and others, unsweetened

Mirin

Orange juice concentrate (frozen)

Pumpkin purée, unsweetened organic (canned)

Rice milk

Soy creamer, plain

Soymilk, plain or vanilla

Tofu, firm, water-packed (14- to 16-ounce packages; keep refrigerated)

Tofu, silken, extra-firm (12.3-ounce aseptic packages; store on a pantry shelf)

Tofu, silken (16-ounce packages; keep refrigerated)

Dry ingredients, flours:

White flour, unbleached (organic is best)

Whole wheat pastry flour (organic is best; sometimes labeled whole grain pastry flour)

Dry ingredients, leaveners, thickeners, flavorings:

Agar flakes

Arrowroot powder

Baking powder, aluminum-free

Baking soda

Carob powder

Chocolate, semisweet and bittersweet bars and chips, nondairy (not milk or white chocolate)

Cocoa powder, unsweetened (Dutch-process and natural)

Coconut, unsweetened shredded dried

Cornstarch, organic

Kuzu (optional)

Oats, organic rolled, not quick-cooking (store in the refrigerator or freezer)

Sea salt, finely ground (coarse salt does not dissolve well; table salt can be used)

Spices:

Cinnamon, ground and whole

Cloves, ground

Ginger, ground

Nutmeg, whole (grate with a fine grater)

Turmeric

Fruit:

Dried, sulfite-free:
Apricots
Cranberries
Currants
Dates
Prunes
Raisins
Fresh seasonal

Nut butters:

Almond

Cashew

Peanut

Nuts and seeds, whole raw (store in the refrigerator or freezer):

Almonds

Cashews

Pecan halves

Pignoli (pine nuts)

Pumpkin seeds

Sesame seeds

Sunflower seeds

Walnut halves

Natural Sweeteners

The average American consumes more than 130 pounds of sugar a year. According to the United States Department of Agriculture this includes naturally occurring sugars in fruits, vegetables, milk (lactose), grains, and beans. But by far, the largest percentage is the sugar that is added to prepared foods. Breakfast cereals, breads, canned and frozen foods, ketchup, fries, and sodas are foods that are particularly high in sugar. Even nonfoods contain sugar or artificial sweeteners. These include toothpaste, table salt, and cigarettes. When you read labels and see words ending in "ose," such as high-fructose corn syrup and maltose, you have found sugar.

Raw sugarcane contains only 14 percent sucrose before it is refined to 99 percent pure crystalline sucrose, which is one of the simple sugars. When simple sugar is consumed, it enters the bloodstream faster than it can be assimilated. The body responds by releasing a burst of insulin from the pancreas. This causes glucose levels to drop, resulting in the irritability or fatigue many people experience after eating or drinking sugary foods. The body then craves more sugar to help elevate the glucose levels, and thus the cycle continues. Unlike refined white sugar, natural sweeteners retain some fiber and nutrients, are digested more slowly, are processed without chemicals, and may be organically grown.

I do not propose that sugar is a health food, but organic, less-refined sugars are superior to refined sugars. Sugarcane is heavily sprayed with pesticides and herbicides, hurtful to sugarcane workers, consumers, and the planet. Organic sugars and sweeteners are always the best choice and worth the slight added cost.

Conventionally refined white sugar, whether from cane or beets, is pure white because all the natural molasses has been extracted out of the cane. It is 99 percent pure sucrose. Raw cane sugar is made snowy white by repeated processing, not by chemical bleaching, but often by filtering it through bone char, a refining process that is not acceptable to vegetarians and vegans. Most conventional brown sugar is "painted sugar," white sugar that has been sprayed with brown-colored syrup.

Molasses is a by-product of sugar refining, and the pesticide residues found in sugarcane remain in molasses after it has been processed. The good news is that organic molasses is available in natural food markets, and I am happily using it again.

Maple syrup and maple sugar are the most natural and least refined natural sweeteners and have been used for hundreds of years. Maple syrup is nothing more than the boiled sap of maple trees. Maple sugar is evaporated, granulated maple syrup. Native Americans introduced maple syrup and maple sugar to colonists who dubbed it "Indian sugar." Maple was cheap and remained the primary sweetener in this country until the mid-nineteenth century. The exorbitant cost of white sugar made it a luxury item afforded only by the wealthy. Times have changed and the prices of white sugar and maple sweetener have reversed. Buying maple syrup in bulk quantities (see page 210) lowers the cost considerably. To prevent fermentation and mold, store your maple syrup in the freezer (it does not freeze solid).

A number of different sweeteners are specified in the recipes in this book. Both granulated (dry) and liquid sweeteners are used, but one type cannot be substituted for the other. For example, one cup of maple syrup used in place of one cup of maple sugar would result in a batter that was too wet; if the substitution were reversed, the batter would be too dry.

Natural sweeteners range from less refined to nearly whole. Each natural sweetener has its own distinctive flavor and color. Light colored light natural cane sugars have just a hint of molasses, while molasses is more clearly evident in dark whole cane sugar. The difference in color and flavor will also be apparent in the finished recipe, so take this into consideration when deciding which sweetener to use. When I give a choice of sweeteners in a list of ingredients, they are listed in order of preference for that particular recipe.

The following is a description of the most readily available sweeteners, both granulated (dry) and liquid. There's no standard terminology used by the food industry for natural granulated sweeteners, so manufacturers sometimes use different names for the same product. For instance, some brands of dark whole cane sugar (such as Sucanat and Rapadura) are labeled "evaporated cane juice," a confusing term, as it might lead you to think the product is a liquid sweetener and not dry granules. After consulting with many students and readers, I've decided on the terms "dark whole cane sugar" and "light natural cane sugar" to distinguish among the many types and brands now in the marketplace. Whichever brand of sweetener you choose, do select an organic type over one that is nonorganic.

Granulated (Dry) Sweeteners

Maple sugar is maple syrup that has been evaporated. Because it tastes like maple syrup, it is perfect in some recipes and not advisable in others. It is expensive and best purchased in bulk.

Dark whole cane sugar is found in one- or five-pound packages and in bulk bins. It ranges in color from medium to dark brown, and though granulated, it is coarse. This sweetener is processed from the juice of the whole sugarcane and the molasses is retained. Dark whole cane sugar is the wrong choice when a dessert with a light color is desirable, and it does taste of molasses. I recommend grinding it to a finer consistency in a blender before storing it in a tightly closed jar or container.

Light natural cane sugar is widely available and is the closest in taste to white sugar. It ranges from very light to a medium beige color and from finely granulated to more coarse. It is a good choice when a traditional taste and color is preferred. It is found in one- or five-pound packages and in the bulk bins of many markets.

Date sugar is made from grinding dried dates. It does not dissolve well and burns easily. Reserve date sugar for sprinkling on puddings, crisps, and similar desserts.

Artificial sweeteners should never be used; they are chemicals, not foods.

Liquid Sweeteners

Liquid sweeteners have very different tastes and consistencies, and substitutions will result in poor, or at least unpredictable, results. Sometimes a combination of liquid sweeteners is used in a recipe.

Maple syrup is my favorite liquid sweetener. Dark amber is the most widely available and perfect for most desserts. Buy it in bulk when possible; you can keep containers of syrup in your freezer for months. It becomes more viscous but does not freeze solid.

Brown rice syrup has a lovely mild caramel taste and is thick and sticky. Cookies made entirely with rice syrup are often too hard or sticky, but they develop a nice crispness if made with rice syrup in combination with another sweetener. Cakes and muffins made with brown rice syrup are too sticky, damp, and heavy. Note that warm brown rice syrup is easier to measure and mix with other ingredients (see page 34).

Barley malt syrup and *organic molasses* have strong flavors that enhance pumpkin and sweet potato pie, spice cake, and sauces. A little goes a long way, and they are best used in combination with mildly flavored sweeteners. As with brown rice syrup, these are thick and sticky and should be liquefied by heating before measuring.

Honey is a food produced by bees and is 1¼ times as sweet as white sugar. Honey should never be fed to children under two years of age because botulism is a risk. A vegan diet does not include honey.

Concentrated fruit sweeteners are not recommended. They are highly processed refined sources of sugar. Virtually non of the fruit from which they are derived remains. Concentrated fruit juice is essentially simple sugar, and the concentrates are routinely deionized to prevent fermentation. This is an example of the importance of considering the type and amount of processing used in food production. Reducing good quality all-fruit juices by simmering to make them more concentrated will give you the best fruit sweetener.

Corn syrup, also known as glucose syrup, is a highly refined food made from cornstarch. High-fructose corn syrup, an ingredient in many processed foods, is sweeter than sucrose and cheap to produce.

Liquid sweeteners are humectants, meaning they contribute and hold moisture. This is a plus, as less fat is needed, baked goods tend to be moister, and staling is retarded.

Fats

Fat is the generic term for butter, margarine, vegetable shortening, lard, and oils. The fat used in all the recipes in this book is neutral-flavored, expeller-pressed canola oil (organic if possible). Fat-phobes beware: fat-free baked goods are made with extra sugar, generally have textures like rubber, and are not satisfying (to most of us). We usually respond to the lack of fat by eating more of these sugar-laden treats. Fat-reduced baked goods, on the other hand, made with limited amounts of good quality fat, are satisfying and delicious. The fat in the recipes in this book is kept to a minimum, but if you need to keep your fat intake to the absolute minimum, choose naturally fat-free, delicious fruit desserts and gels.

Good quality oils are extracted without the use of solvents or chemicals. The oils are sensitive to light and heat, and should be stored in the refrigerator or freezer.

Margarine was once thought to be the great cholesterol-free alternative to butter, but it is actually a liquid oil transformed through the process of hydrogenation into solid fat. Hydrogenation creates trans fats, which actually raise levels of LDL (bad) cholesterol and lower HDL (good) cholesterol. I do not use or recommend the use of soy margarine.

Flours

The recipes in this book list **unbleached white flour**, and while that is the best choice, you can substitute the same amount of all-purpose flour.

Whole wheat pastry flour (sometimes labeled whole grain flour) is not the all-purpose whole wheat flour you generally see on supermarket shelves, which is good for making breads but not pastries. Use organic flours when possible, and keep them cool to protect the oils in the germ from becoming rancid. Refrigerate or freeze whole grain flours in tightly closed containers or zipper-lock plastic bags for up to three months. Using a combination of whole wheat pastry flour and unbleached white flour in a 50/50 ratio creates baked goods with a great crumb and texture.

Spelt flour is tolerated by some of the individuals who are allergic or sensitive to wheat. Substitute the same quantity of spelt flour, using half white spelt flour and half whole grain spelt flour for the best result, as listed in the recipe. If you can only find whole grain spelt flour, which is labeled simply "spelt flour," your baked goods will be somewhat heavier than those made with a combination of white and whole grain, but nice nonetheless.

Leaveners

Baking soda is bicarbonate of soda. It leavens dough by releasing bubbles of carbon dioxide when mixed with an acid, such as vinegar.

Baking powder is baking soda plus an acid, such as cream of tartar. Purchase double acting, aluminum-free baking powder, whenever possible. Vinegar mixed with baking powder creates bubbles of carbon dioxide that help the batter rise, and this reaction neutralizes the acidic flavor of the vinegar. Vinegar also tenderizes the gluten in flour to help produce a cake with a fine crumb, particularly cakes made without eggs. I use unfiltered, unpasteurized apple cider vinegar and store it in the refrigerator.

Chocolate

Chocolate is the new wine, or so say many foodies. Single origin chocolates, extra-bitter chocolates, and chocolate bars listing antioxidants as ingredients are all the latest rage. I am happy to report much more organic and fair trade chocolate has come to market.

Studies indicate that the phenolic acids present in chocolate provide antioxidant benefits, that its stearic acids help raise HDL (good) cholesterol, and that chocolate boosts serotonin levels, which brightens moods. I have met very few people who do not like chocolate. I have met people, on the other hand, who consider chocolate to be one of the four food groups. Properly made chocolate melts in your hands as well as your mouth and continues to be one of the most popular foods in the world.

Chocolate comes from beans that grow inside the pods of cacao trees, which are among the oldest trees on earth. Chocolate's flavor, color, and aroma develop after the beans have been fermented, roasted, and ground into a paste. Chocolate liquor (not an alcoholic ingredient), an element of the paste, contains a fat called cocoa butter, which is nondairy.

How to Melt Chocolate

Melt chocolate slowly over low heat; there is no remedy for scorched chocolate. Use a serrated knife to chop the chocolate into small pieces. Place the chocolate in a metal bowl set over a saucepan of very hot water. Make certain the water does not touch the bottom of the bowl. Bring the water to a boil and immediately turn off the heat. Stir the chocolate gently with a rubber spatula from time to time until it has melted.

Cocoa

Cocoa is the dry, bitter powder remaining after the chocolate liquor is partially defatted. Cocoa provides a concentrated taste and works beautifully in nondairy, egg-free recipes. Most cocoa powder ranges from 10 to 20 percent fat. Compare this with the minimum fat content of solid chocolate (54 percent), and you can see why cocoa powder is an asset in lower-fat desserts. The recipes in this book use only unsweetened cocoa powder, primarily Dutch-process cocoa, always unsweetened.

In the early nineteenth century, Dutchman Coenraad Johannes van Houten discovered that the acid taste of cocoa was neutralized if he added alkali-potash to the nibs before they were roasted. Ever since the end of the nineteenth century, many chocolate makers have practiced this alkalization process to modify the flavor and the color of the final product. Another technical term for alkalization still used today is "Dutch-process" or "Dutching." This type of cocoa is specified in most of the recipes in this book and is referred to as Dutch-process cocoa.

Dutch-process cocoa is sometimes referred to as Dutched, European, alkalized, and other indications. Most imported cocoa powder is Dutch-process. It is darker, smoother in flavor, and less acidic than natural cocoa, which is lighter in color and untreated. Dutch-process cocoa creates the best result. If you cannot get Dutch-process cocoa, you can substitute natural cocoa in baking recipes (add a pinch of baking soda), though the outcome will be slightly different. However, natural cocoa is not acceptable in recipes for frostings, whips, creams, puddings, and desserts that are uncooked. The taste will be disappointing. Organic Dutch-process and natural cocoa powders (some are fair trade as well) are available in most natural food markets and by mail order (see page 210). Hershey's makes both natural and Dutch-process cocoa powder; Droste cocoa powder is Dutch-process and available in most supermarkets. Neither brand is organic. Some of the other more widely available organic brands are Green & Black's (Dutch-process), Rapunzel (natural), and Equal Exchange (Dutch-process, though there is no indication on the can).

Pesticides have been routinely used in the production of chocolate, but when cocoa is not sprayed with pesticides, the farmers working on it don't suffer from the health-related problems that typically plague farmers who grow cocoa conventionally. With organically grown cocoa, pesticides don't end up in the chocolate we eat and they don't pollute our environment. When you buy certified fair trade chocolate (or coffee or tea), you are enabling farmers to live with dignity and invest in their families, communities, and the environment. Spread the word to your friends, family, and coworkers, and help sow the seeds for a better life for producers and their families around the world.

Carob

Like chocolate, *carob* (also known as St. John's bread) comes from the pod of a tropical tree. Chocolate and carob are not generally interchangeable, although many recipes indicate otherwise. Both carob powder and natural cocoa powder are light brown in color. That is where the similarity ends.

Carob should be appreciated and savored for its own distinctive, sweet taste. To compare the flavor of carob to that of chocolate is like expecting tofu to taste like tempeh or yogurt like heavy cream.

Carob is derived from the dried, roasted, ground pods of the Mediterranean honey locust tree. Carob contains very little fat, is caffeine free, and contains a good dose of calcium and pectin. It has enjoyed a reputation as a food superior to chocolate. However, carob contains more than 40 percent naturally occurring sugars. Most important, many of the carob confections found in the marketplace contain hydrogenated oils and sometimes dairy. The fat and sugar content of some manufactured carob candies is as high as sugar-sweetened, dairy-laden conventional chocolate bars. Read those labels, my fellow consumers, and let the buyer beware.

Nuts, Seeds, and Oats

The flavor and digestibility of nuts, seeds, and oats will be enhanced if they are lightly crisped in the oven. Preheat the oven to 325 degrees (unless the recipe you're following specifies differently). Spread the nuts in a single layer on a baking sheet lined with parchment paper, and bake for 5 to 7 minutes, just until they become fragrant and hot. Check them after 5 minutes and again every minute after that to prevent burning. Nuts can go from fragrant to burnt in seconds, and they darken and crisp further as they cool. Toast seeds following the directions for toasting nuts, but use a cooler oven (300 degrees) and toast them for 5 to 6 minutes only. Rolled oats can be toasted in the oven using the same method and timing as for nuts.

Nuts, seeds, and oats must be cool before they are chopped or ground. Nuts are high in good-quality fat and can become rancid quickly; store raw nuts in a covered container or zipper-lock plastic bag in the refrigerator or freezer.

Coconut

Unsweetened dried coconut is far superior to the much-too-sugary grated coconut found in packages in the baking aisle of the supermarket. Toasting unsweetened dried coconut brings out its nutty, tropical flavor. Preheat the oven to 300 degrees and line a baking sheet with parchment paper. Spread the coconut in one layer on the sheet and toast for 10 to 15 minutes, stirring every 5 minutes, until the coconut is golden brown, being careful not to let the coconut burn. Let cool completely. Store the toasted coconut in an airtight container in the refrigerator or freezer for up to two months.

Agar

Gelatin-based desserts, also known as jellies, gelées, aspics, blancmanges, and molds, are combinations of a liquid (usually fruit juice, milk, or wine) and a gelling agent. Fruit is often added to these desserts, which makes them infinitely variable.

Hundreds of years ago, the gelling agent cooks used was a pure, flavorless protein extracted from animal bones, feet, cartilage, and tendons. The process was labor intensive and lengthy, so gelatin-based foods were found only on the tables of wealthy families. In 1889, Charles B. Knox introduced packaged powdered bovine gelatin. Boxes of nearly instant, sugary, brightly colored powder followed, and gelatin creations became popular additions to the family meal. My family's specialty—a square of green gel mixed with canned, crushed pineapple—was served on a lettuce leaf. I liked to play with the wobbly gel, but wouldn't eat it. Fortunately agar—a natural, colorless, and flavorless gelling agent derived from sea vegetables and rich in iodine, calcium, phosphorous, and trace elements—is widely available and easy to use. Agar (also called agar-agar and kanten) is found in three forms: flakes, bars, and powder. Agar powder is highly processed and concentrated, and has an unpleasant taste that is apparent in the finished dish. I do not recommend it; but for reference, the powder has five times the gelling power of agar flakes. Agar flakes are the most readily available, and they are the easiest to measure and cook with. Agar flakes are used almost exclusively in the recipes in this book.

Although I often hear frustrated students and chefs complain that agar flakes are difficult to dissolve, that's really not the case if you follow a few practical tips. Adhere to these simple "rules" and your gels and creamy desserts will be perfect every time.

Note: Before you begin any recipes for these desserts, read them all the way through and make sure you understand the instructions.

Agar Flakes

1. Soak agar flakes briefly in cool liquid prior to cooking. This is the secret to dissolving them easily and thoroughly. At least 10 minutes before you begin cooking, measure the agar into a saucepan, pour in the liquid specified in the recipe, and allow the agar to soak and soften. Do not stir or heat the liquid while the agar is soaking. (This is the same process as letting gelatin "bloom.") I have found that agar does not dissolve thoroughly in soymilk, rice milk, or nut milks, so I recommend using water or juice in most cases. As a general rule, 1 tablespoon of agar flakes gels 1 cup of liquid, but working with any type of gelatin is not an exact science. Certain ingredients (citrus and pineapple, for example) weaken the gel, and when they are used, more agar is needed. (See Agar Equivalents, page 26.)

2. After the agar has soaked, cover the saucepan with a lid, and bring the liquid to a boil over medium heat. Pay close attention, as the liquid has a tendency to boil over. When the liquid reaches a boil, reduce the heat to low, uncover, and stir well to mix in any agar floating in the liquid or stuck on the bottom of the saucepan. Cover and simmer for 7 to 10 minutes, stirring once or twice. Remove a large spoonful of liquid and look for any specks of agar. If necessary, simmer a little longer, until the agar is dissolved, checking every minute or two.

3. If you have the time, I suggest you test the texture of the agar mixture before you finish cooking the recipe to make sure what you get at serving time is what you expect. To do this, place a tablespoon of gel on a chilled spoon and refrigerate it for 5 to 10 minutes; it should set up to the consistency of conventional gelatin. If the gel is too hard, add more liquid to your recipe; if it is too soft, soak additional agar in a little liquid (use Agar Equivalents, page 26, as a guide). Then add it to the saucepan and cook to dissolve. Cool the gel until it is slightly thicker before adding other ingredients such as sliced fruit or berries.

Agar Bars

Soak agar bars in a bowl of room temperature water for 1 or 2 minutes, until soft. Squeeze to remove the excess water, tear into pieces, and add to the liquid specified in the recipe. Proceed with the recipe as directed.

Agar Equivalents

After several years of testing, I have learned that agar flakes and conventional bovine gelatin can be used almost interchangeably (use heaping teaspoons of agar flakes to replace level teaspoons of bovine gelatin).

• Use 3 teaspoons (1 tablespoon) of agar flakes…	to gel 1 cup of liquid.
• When citrus is a main ingredient…	use 10 to 15 percent more agar.
• 4 tablespoons (¼ cup) agar flakes…	equals 1 bar agar.
• 2¼ teaspoons (one ¼-ounce packet) of conventional bovine gelatin…	gels 1 cup of liquid.
• 1¼-ounce packet of conventional bovine gelatin…	equals 5 sheets (leaves) of gelatin.

Arrowroot, Cornstarch, and Kuzu

Arrowroot, cornstarch, and kuzu are three types of starch that thicken and contribute a creamy texture to nondairy, egg-free desserts. All must be thoroughly dissolved in cool liquid prior to being added to the mixture being cooked. Dissolved starch is referred to as a slurry.

Arrowroot is a powdered starch made from a tropical tuber. It is similar to cornstarch in appearance, but once cooked it is clear and shiny rather than cloudy and translucent. This makes arrowroot a better choice for brightly colored fruit sauces, although cornstarch works well in chocolate or carob pudding and apple pie. Purchase arrowroot in bulk packages available in natural food stores, spice and herb shops, and from mail order sources (see page 210). The small bottles of arrowroot found on supermarket shelves are extremely expensive.

Cornstarch can be used in place of arrowroot with no change in measurement, but cornstarch-thickened mixtures must be cooked about 30 seconds after they boil.

Kuzu is a high-quality starch made from the root of the kuzu plant that grows wild in the mountains of Japan. Like arrowroot, it makes shiny, translucent sauces. Kuzu is said to be excellent for digestion and a cure for gastric inflammation, but considering its prohibitive cost, it makes sense to save this root for recipes where its medicinal properties are valued. Kuzu is lumpy—you can crush the lumps before measuring it, or you can measure it by rounded spoonfuls. It has twice the thickening power of arrowroot and cornstarch, so half as much is needed. Kuzu-thickened mixtures must cook for 1 minute after they boil.

Arrowroot and cornstarch equivalents for thickening 1 cup liquid

- 1 tablespoon equals 1/4 ounce.

- 1 ounce equals 4 tablespoons (1/4 cup).

- *To make a thin sauce*, use 1/2 tablespoon (1 1/2 teaspoons) arrowroot or cornstarch dissolved in 1 tablespoon liquid.

- *To make a medium sauce*, use 1 tablespoon arrowroot or cornstarch dissolved in 1 1/2 tablespoons liquid.

- *To make a thick sauce*, use 2 tablespoons arrowroot or cornstarch dissolved in 2 1/2 tablespoons liquid.

Note: As with agar, when citrus is an ingredient, 10 to 15 percent more arrowroot may be needed.

Cooking with Starch

1. Measure the specified starch into a small bowl and mix with the cool liquid called for in the recipe. Stir with a fork to dissolve. The dissolved starch is now referred to as a slurry.

2. Always stir the slurry with a fork once more, just before cooking, since the starch settles to the bottom. Wait until the mixture you are cooking is simmering before adding the slurry; stir constantly with a wire whisk as you pour it in.

The mixture will look cloudy at this point, but will clear and thicken when it is close to boiling. Continue to whisk slowly until a full boil is reached. Remove arrowroot-thickened mixtures from the heat as soon as they boil. Further cooking or stirring may cause the mixture to thin out. Cook cornstarch-thickened mixtures 30 to 60 seconds longer; kuzu-thickened mixtures must boil for a full minute.

Tofu

Tofu, also known as bean curd, is made from curdled soymilk. It is sometimes referred to as "the vegetable cow" because it provides all the essential protein that humans need for growth, and is a good source of B vitamins and iron. But unlike cows, tofu contains no cholesterol and is low in saturated fat. It is perishable and should be kept refrigerated, unless it is the type of tofu that comes in aseptic boxes, which need no refrigeration until opened.

Tofu has a flavor that ranges from nutty and somewhat "beany" to quite neutral, depending upon the type and manufacturer. Tofu is often available packed in water in sealed plastic containers and sold in the dairy sections of most supermarkets, natural food stores, and Asian markets. The packages range in size from 15 to 19 ounces, and are available in several textures: soft, firm, extra-firm. The texture is determined by the amount of water used to make the tofu.

A note about the fresh tofu that is sold in bulk out of open containers: fresh tofu is found mainly in ethnic markets and I never buy it. I find myself wondering about the freshness and cleanliness, but if you are sure of your source, it is an option. Make sure you blanch it before using.

Using Tofu in Desserts

Only two types of tofu are used in the recipes in this book: firm tofu (which I refer to in recipes simply as tofu) and silken tofu. They are not interchangeable, but if you cannot find silken tofu, soft regular tofu can be substituted.

• **Silken tofu** is a custard-like product, found in either 12.3-ounce aseptic boxes (labeled soft, firm, or extra-firm) or 16-ounce refrigerated packages (labled simply silken tofu with no firmness designated). When I choose tofu in aseptic boxes, I use firm or extra-firm. To use, open the package and drain off any liquid in the container. Refrigerated tofu should be drained for at least 12 hours before using by placing it in a strainer set over a bowl. Cover with plastic wrap and refrigerate up to a day ahead. Use the drained liquid when you make smoothies.

• **Soft tofu** is usually found in 14- to 16-ounce packages in the dairy section of supermarkets or natural food stores. If you cannot find silken tofu, use soft tofu. Drain it for a few hours before using.

• **Regular tofu** is dense and solid. Firm tofu should be blanched in simmering water prior to using. This step freshens the tofu and reduces its "beany" flavor.

To blanch regular tofu, pour 6 quarts of water into a saucepan and add ½ teaspoon of salt. Bring the water to a boil over high heat. Remove the saucepan from the heat and add the tofu. Allow the tofu to remain in the water for 4 to 5 minutes. Lift the tofu out of the water with a strainer and cool to room temperature. Use immediately in a recipe or refrigerate the tofu in a covered container for up to three days. If you use tofu often, it pays to blanch a few blocks at the same time. Drain off any liquid that has accumulated in the container before you proceed with the recipe.

Try to use organic tofu; most soybeans are genetically engineered and heavily sprayed with pesticides.

Essential Equipment

Healthy baking does not require fancy equipment. My big electric mixer sits on a shelf, replaced by bowls and hand whisks.

Aluminum cookware is widely used in the food service industry, despite the fact that aluminum contamination has been linked to a wide range of health problems. Better choices for cooks are stainless steel (a layer of aluminum sandwiched on the bottom is common and desirable), tinned steel, glass and ceramic pie pans and baking dishes, and enameled and plain cast iron. Similarly, aluminum foil should not touch food directly. Use it only to overwrap parchment-covered baking dishes.

Purchasing good quality pots, pans, and tools is well worth the cost. They perform better and make cooking and baking a pleasure. Using inadequate tools is frustrating and can spoil your efforts. Heavy cookie sheets and baking pans do not warp in a hot oven, and pots with heavy bottoms help to keep foods from scorching. Excellent quality pots and pans go on sale several times a year.

Use the Correct Size Baking Pans

Too little batter in a too big pan equals a cake that is dry and thin. Too much batter in a pan that is too small yields a cake that does not cook through. The center will be wet and gummy and will most likely collapse.

It is safe to assume that unless a recipe indicates otherwise, the proper volume of nondairy batter to use is one-third to a scant half the depth of the pan. Cakes are expected to rise.

In order to substitute one baking pan for another, the volume of the new pan must be equal to the one originally called for in a recipe. You can determine the volume of any pan by using a liquid measuring cup filled with water to fill the pan. Pans are measured across the top from rim to rim.

- A round cake pan holds three-quarters the volume of the same size square pan.

- For an 8-inch round pan, use $1\frac{1}{2}$ to 2 cups batter.

- For a 9-inch round pan, use 2 to 3 cups batter.

- For a 9 x 9-inch square pan, use 3 to 4 cups batter.

- For a 9 x 13-inch pan (sheet cake), use 6 to 8 cups batter.

- For a 9-inch heart-shaped pan, use 2 to $2\frac{1}{2}$ cups batter.

Other Equipment

Everything you need to make and bake all the recipes in this book is in this list. Buy individual items as needed, but remember, if you buy cheap equipment, you'll be buying trouble.

Paring knives, one or two

Chef's knife, 9 or 10 inch (keep your knives sharp)

Serrated knife (sometimes called a baker's knife)

Cutting boards, wood, dedicated to desserts (no garlic)

Kitchen scissors

Vegetable peelers

Wire mesh strainers, medium (use instead of sifters)

Saucepans and covers, 1 quart, 2 quart, 3 quart, and 8 quart

Measuring cups and spoons, liquid and dry measures

Mixing bowls, small, medium, large, stainless steel and glass

Flexible rubber spatulas, small, medium, large

Wire whisks, small, medium, large

Mixing spoons, stainless steel and wood

Microplane zester

Pastry brushes, several (for oiling pans and glazing baked goods)

Cake testers or skewers

Wire cooling racks, rounds, squares, and a large rectangle

Offset (angled) metal spatulas (also called icing spatulas), small and medium

Rolling pin, heavy with a ball bearing handle (or your favorite type)

Food processor

Blender

Oven thermometer (I keep two in my oven)

Oven timer (triple timers are invaluable)

Parchment paper (also called baker's paper)

Standard muffin tin, 6 cup or 12 cup (cups 2½ to 2¾ inches wide x 1 to 1½ inches deep)

Square baking pans, 8 and 9 inch

Round cake pans, two or more, 8 and 9 inch

Springform pans, 9 x 3 inch

Tart pans with removable bottoms, 8 and 9 inch

Pie pans, 8 and 9 inch

Baking pans, 9 x 13 inch

Loaf pans: 8½ x 4½ x 2½ inch (6-cup capacity) and 9 x 5 x 3 inch (8-cup capacity)

Note: These are the most common pan sizes. The recipe will state which size pan to use. You can use Pyrex pans or metal pans.

Cake-decorating turntable

Cardboard cake rounds, 8 and 9 inch

Cookie sheets (optional)

Baking sheets with shallow rims (also called half sheet pans), light colored

Kitchen towels

Oven mitts

Storage containers

Food wrap and bags

Cake and pie servers

Pastry bag and tips (optional)

Tips and Techniques for Making and Baking Desserts

Please read this short but important section carefully. More specific information on how to make specific categories of desserts—cookies, quick-mix desserts, cakes, pies, and tarts—is found in the individual chapters.

Baking is said to be challenging, encumbered by delicate and precise techniques and unforgiving ingredients, but really, this is not at all the case. Believe me, if a degree in chemistry were required of a pastry chef, I'd be doing something else. The longer I make desserts, the more convinced I am that the process is predictable as well as creative, so don't obsess or stress, but do heed the following four keys to successful dessert making.

1. Accuracy is key to a predictable outcome. Measure ingredients carefully and check the oven temperature.

2. The proper equipment is essential, but nothing out of the ordinary is needed to make the recipes in this book. These recipes have been created for the home cook and tested in an ordinary oven (though I'd love a new convection wall oven).

3. High-quality, fresh ingredients make the best tasting desserts.

4. Think like a pastry chef: Organize your mise en place. Mise en place (pronounced MEEZ ahn plahs) is translated as "to put in place." It means simply to have all your ingredients prepared and ready to go before you start cooking.

A Baker's Dozen Secrets to Successful Desserts

1. Read the entire recipe carefully all the way through to avoid any unpleasant surprises. (For example, you drained the fruit and discarded the juice in step two but, oops, the juice was needed in step four.) Make sure you understand all the steps.

2. Position one or more oven racks in the correct section of the oven as noted in the recipe. Cakes and cookies bake best on the middle rack and pies and tarts on the lowest.

3. Always preheat the oven to the temperature specified in the recipe before mixing the batter, and check the temperature with an oven thermometer (available at supermarkets, kitchenware stores, and hardware stores). If the thermometer reads 375 degrees and you need to bake at 325

degrees, reduce the temperature by 50 degrees and check again. No two ovens are alike; get to know yours.

4. Organize your ingredients for baking. Gather all the ingredients and prepare them as needed: toast, cool, and chop the nuts; warm the rice syrup; blanch the tofu; chill the oil; soak the agar. You don't want to find that you're missing an ingredient midway through preparing a recipe.

5. Use good-quality ingredients: pure vanilla extract, not vanillin, which is artificial flavoring; pure maple syrup, not pancake syrup; fresh flour (organic is best); aluminum-free baking powder (date the can when you open it; baking powder stays fresh about three months). Store ingredients properly. Whole grains and unrefined flours, nuts, seeds, oils, and maple syrup should be refrigerated or frozen in covered containers or zipper-lock plastic bags.

6. Select the correct size pan. If the pan is too big or too small for the amount of batter, your cake will be either thin and burnt or overflowing and gooey. To find the volume of any pan, fill it with water, and carefully pour the water out into a measuring cup. To ensure that the center bakes through, nondairy, egg-free cake batters generally do not fill the pan more than a scant half full, unless the recipe specifies differently.

7. Use a pastry brush dipped in canola oil to grease the bottom and sides of the baking pan, and line the bottom of the pan with a piece of parchment paper cut to fit. You want your cakes to come out of the pan in one piece.

8. Measure the dry and liquid ingredients accurately using the correct utensil for each. Use straight-sided cups to measure dry ingredients by the dip-and-sweep method. Dip a cup made for dry ingredients into the flour, for example, and scoop up a heaping cupful. Do not pack or shake the flour. Place the cup over waxed paper or parchment paper (not over the mixing bowl), and level the top with the straight side of a knife. Measure all other dry ingredients (granulated sweeteners and cocoa, for example) in straight-sided cups using this method and measure smaller amounts such as salt, baking powder, baking soda, and dry spices in the same way using measuring spoons. After the dry ingredients are measured, place them in a wire

mesh strainer set over a mixing bowl in order to sift them. Tap the strainer against the palm of your hand to sift the ingredients into the bowl.

To measure liquid ingredients, use a glass or plastic cup with a pouring spout. Place the cup on a flat surface, pour in the specified amount of liquid, and lean down until you are eye level to check the amount. When measuring less than one cup of liquid, a one-cup measure is the most accurate.

9. Heating thick, sticky brown rice syrup, barley malt, and molasses before they are measured makes working with them much easier. Place an open jar or container of the sweetener in a saucepan of water and bring the water to a simmer over low heat. Stir the syrup once or twice and warm it until it has begun to liquefy. When you have measured what you need, cool, cover, and refrigerate the rest.

10. Never, ever combine dry and liquid ingredients until you are certain the oven temperature is correct and the pans are prepared. The leavening action starts as soon as a batter is mixed, and it will dissipate if the prepared batter sits on your counter as you wait for the oven to heat. You don't need to race, but do get batters right in the oven.

11. It may be obvious, but clean up as you go along. Put a large piece of parchment paper on the counter to catch spills and act as a spoon rest. Bake pies on parchment paper–lined baking sheets for easier handling and to catch spillovers.

12. Do not overcrowd the oven. Arrange cake pans about two inches apart and two inches away from the oven walls for even baking.

13. Set a timer and resist the temptation to open the oven door before the minimum baking time has elapsed. Check your baked goods quickly so the oven temperature doesn't drop.

Now, go into the kitchen and bake something yummy!

Chapter 2... Great Good Gels, Creams, Puddings, and Sauces

Introducing Great Good Gels and Creams Naturally

Gels, mousses, puddings, and creams are traditionally made from ingredients that many people no longer want to include in their diets—dairy products such as milk, cream, and butter; eggs; gelatin; and white sugar—but the good news is that we can have our creams and eat them too. The recipes in this chapter range from simple, no-sweetener-added gelled desserts to rich-tasting creamy desserts. The milk, heavy cream, eggs, butter, and white sugar are gone, replaced by healthful ingredients.

The Secrets to Making Nondairy, Egg-Free Gels, Creams, Mousses, Puddings, and Sauces

The secret to making equally delicious and maybe even better tasting versions of conventional desserts is to substitute more healthful alternatives. For example, soymilk or rice milk can be used instead of cow's milk; agar, derived from sea vegetables, easily replaces bovine gelatin; and arrowroot, a quality root starch, and organic cornstarch contribute the creamy texture associated with this category of dessert. Using a small amount of arrowroot in agar-based gels adds a subtle creaminess that is desirable. Tofu replaces cream and sometimes eggs. Tofu-based whipped toppings are delicious, and a variety of natural sweeteners can take the place of refined white sugar.

Better Fruit Gel-Oh

Yield: 4 to 6 servings

4 tablespoons agar flakes

4 cups fruit juice (see page 26)

4 teaspoons arrowroot

4 teaspoons cool water

2 cups fresh berries or sliced fruit

Tips: One agar bar can replace the agar flakes in this recipe. Soften the bar in a bowl of water for 1 to 2 minutes. Squeeze to remove the excess water, tear the bar into pieces, and stir into the juice. Proceed with the recipe as directed in step 1.

• To achieve the firmer texture of commercial gelatin desserts, omit the arrowroot and add 1 additional tablespoon of agar flakes. Proceed with the recipe as directed.

It's easy to avoid the sugar, artificial color, and additives found in packaged gelatin desserts. Make gels instead with organic fruit juice, agar (a natural gelling agent), and arrowroot. Also called kantens, gels are light, satisfying, and 100 percent fat free. Serve plain or with a spoonful of tofu whip (see pages 56–57). Both agar and arrowroot are available in natural food stores, ethnic markets, large supermarkets, and through mail order sources (see page 210).

1. Measure the agar into a medium saucepan. Pour in the juice, but do not stir or heat. Set aside for 10 minutes or longer to allow the agar to soften. (This will help the agar dissolve thoroughly and easily.)

2. Cover the saucepan with a lid and bring the liquid to a boil over medium heat. Uncover, reduce the heat to low, and stir to release any bits of agar that may be stuck on the bottom of the saucepan. Cover and simmer for 7 to 10 minutes, stirring a few times.

3. Uncover and check the juice in the saucepan, examining a large spoonful for specks of agar. If necessary, cover and simmer longer until the agar has completely dissolved.

4. Combine the arrowroot with the water in a small bowl and stir with a fork to dissolve. Add the dissolved arrowroot to the simmering juice mixture, whisking constantly. Cook over medium heat only until the liquid boils. Immediately remove the saucepan from the heat. (If you cook or stir arrowroot-thickened mixtures after they have boiled, they are likely to become thin again.)

5. Pour into a serving bowl or individual dishes. Cool 15 minutes, or until the mixture is beginning to gel. Stir in the fruit, and refrigerate 30 to 40 minutes, until set. Refrigerate leftover gel in a covered container; it will keep for two to three days.

Blueberry Gel

2 cups fresh blueberries, picked over, rinsed, and patted dry (see tip)

3 tablespoons agar flakes

4 cups apple or other fruit juice (see page 26)

2 tablespoons arrowroot

2 tablespoons cool water

Tip: Frozen blueberries can replace fresh berries; simmer 1 to 2 minutes longer and proceed with the recipe.

This gel is slightly softer than the preceding recipe, Better Fruit Gel–Oh (page 37), and has an especially beautiful color. Blueberries are as healthful as they are delicious.

1. Measure the agar into a medium saucepan. Pour in the juice, but do not stir or heat. Set aside for 10 minutes or longer to allow the agar to soften. (This will help the agar dissolve thoroughly and easily.)

2. Cover the saucepan with a lid and bring the liquid to a boil over medium heat. Uncover, reduce the heat to low, and stir to release any bits of agar that may be stuck on the bottom of the saucepan. Cover and simmer for 7 to 10 minutes, stirring a few times.

3. Uncover and check the juice in the saucepan, examining a large spoonful for specks of agar. If necessary, cover and simmer longer, until the agar has completely dissolved. Uncover, stir in the blueberries, and simmer 1 minute.

4. Combine the arrowroot with the water in a small bowl and stir with a fork to dissolve. Add the dissolved arrowroot to the simmering juice mixture, whisking constantly. Cook over medium heat only until the liquid boils. Immediately remove the saucepan from the heat, and stir in the vanilla. (If you cook or stir arrowroot-thickened mixtures after they have boiled, they are likely to become thin again.)

5. Pour into a bowl and cool for 15 minutes. Cover and refrigerate 30 to 40 minutes, or until set.

6. Spoon the gel into a food processor and pulse until creamy and a beautiful bright blue. Pour back into the bowl or individual dishes. Store leftover gel in a covered container. It will keep for two to three days.

Blueberry Sauce:

Purée a portion of the set gel in a blender or food processor with a small amount of juice. Add more juice as needed to achieve the consistency you desire.

How to Choose, Wash, and Store Fresh Blueberries

Blueberries, which are native to North America, are nutritional all-stars. They are low in calories, very high in antioxidants, and, like cranberries, help fend off urinary tract infections. Blueberries are at their best from May through October when they are in season; choose firm, bright berries. Before storing blueberries or any berry, pour them out of their container onto a flat dish and discard any that are moldy or soft. Place the unwashed berries in a paper towel–lined container and store them loosely covered in the refrigerator for about five days. If kept out at room temperature for more than a day, the berries may spoil.

Before using, wash the berries in a bowl of water. Scoop the berries into a strainer and rinse, shaking the strainer gently to remove excess water.

Ripe berries can be frozen, although this will slightly change their texture. Use frozen commercial organic berries when fresh ones are not available or freeze your own during blueberry season.

Softly Gelled Fruit Soup
and Blueberry-Fig Salad

Yield: 4 to 6 servings
See photo facing page 48.

Fruit Soup

3 tablespoons agar flakes

4 cups apple or other fruit juice (see page 26)

½ teaspoon vanilla extract

¼ teaspoon orange extract

Tip: The sugar will draw some delicious concentrated fruit juice out of the berries; drizzle some over the fruit, or use it on cake or pudding.

This very softly gelled fruit soup, served with a salad of figs and blueberries, is an elegant fat–free dessert. It was adapted from Molly O'Neill's recipe published years ago in the New York Times.

1.   To make the soup, measure the agar into a medium saucepan. Pour in the juice but do not heat or stir. Set aside for 10 minutes or longer to allow the agar to soften. (This will help the agar dissolve thoroughly and easily.)

2.   Cover the saucepan with a lid and bring the liquid to a boil over medium heat. Uncover, reduce the heat to low, and stir to release any bits of agar that may be stuck on the bottom of the saucepan. Cover and simmer for 7 to 10 minutes, stirring a few times.

3.   Check the juice in the saucepan, examining a large spoonful for specks of agar. If necessary, cover and simmer longer, until the agar has completely dissolved. Remove the saucepan from the heat and stir in the vanilla and orange extracts.

4.   Pour into serving bowls and refrigerate 40 to 50 minutes, or until softly gelled, while assembling the salad.

Gels, Creams, Puddings, Sauces

Blueberry-Fig Salad

2 cups fresh blueberries,
picked over, rinsed,
and patted dry

4 fresh figs, washed and
halved or quartered

1 to 2 tablespoons light
natural cane sugar

¼ teaspoon ground
nutmeg

1 tablespoon finely
grated orange zest

1 to 2 tablespoons
Grand Marnier
(optional)

1 cup Silken Cashew
Cream (page 60)

Orange zest, in long
thin strips, for garnish

5. To make the salad, combine the blueberries, figs, sugar, nutmeg, grated orange zest, and Grand Marnier, if using, in a medium bowl and mix gently. Set aside at room temperature for 30 minutes, or refrigerate up to 4 hours ahead in a covered container.

6. Serve the fruit soup topped with Blueberry-Fig Salad and some of the accumulated fruit juice. Drizzle each serving with a few tablespoons of Silken Cashew Cream and garnish with strips of zest.

Seasonal Fruit Salad:

Substitute an equal quantity of other seasonal fruits for the blueberries and figs.

Mango Pineapple Mousse

Yield: 6 to 8 servings

6 ounces unsweetened dried mango

3 ounces unsweetened dried pineapple

2 to 3 cups mango or apple juice

¼ cup agar flakes

1 (12.3-ounce) box firm or extra-firm silken tofu (1⅓ cups)

2 ripe bananas

2 tablespoons orange juice

½ teaspoon vanilla extract

¼ teaspoon lemon extract

4 teaspoons arrowroot

3 tablespoons cool water

Orange zest, in long thin strips, for garnish

Because drying fruit concentrates the natural fruit sugar, it is not necessary to add additional sweetener to this rich-tasting mousse. Serve in stemmed glass dishes for a festive presentation.

1. Cut the mango and pineapple into small pieces (see tip) and put each fruit into a separate bowl.

2. Pour 2 cups of the mango juice into a medium saucepan and bring to a boil. Pour 1 cup of hot juice into each bowl of fruit and soak about 1 hour until softened. (Drier fruit will take longer to soften; you may find it more convenient to allow the fruit to soak 8 to 12 hours in the refrigerator.)

3. To make the mousse, place the mango and its soaking juice in a food processor and purée until smooth. Keep the puréed mango in the food processor.

4. Drain the pineapple, reserving the soaking juice, and set the pineapple aside. Add enough additional mango juice or water to the soaking juice to measure 1¼ cups. Measure the agar into a medium saucepan. Pour in the juice, but do not stir or heat. Set aside for 10 minutes or longer to allow the agar to soften. (This will help the agar dissolve thoroughly and easily.)

5. Cover the saucepan with a lid and bring the liquid to a boil over medium heat. Uncover, reduce the heat to low, and stir to release any bits of agar that may be stuck on the bottom of the saucepan. Cover and simmer for 7 to 10 minutes, stirring a few times.

Gels, Creams, Puddings, Sauces

6.   Uncover and check the juice in the saucepan, examining a large spoonful for specks of agar. If necessary, cover and simmer longer until the agar has completely dissolved. Cover and keep warm over low heat.

7.   Add the soaked pineapple, tofu, 1 banana, the orange juice, and the vanilla and lemon extracts to the mango purée, and process until smooth.

8.   Combine the arrowroot with the water in a small bowl, and stir with a fork to dissolve. Bring the pineapple juice back to a simmer. Add the dissolved arrowroot to the simmering juice mixture, whisking constantly. The mixture will be very thick and may sputter rather than bubble when it boils. Cook over medium heat only until the liquid boils, then immediately remove from the heat. (If you cook or stir arrowroot-thickened mixtures after they have boiled, they are likely to become thin again.)

9.   Add the hot juice mixture to the food processor and pulse a few times to blend; then process for 1 minute, or until the mousse is smooth. Transfer to a shallow dish, cover, and refrigerate for 50 to 60 minutes, until set, or up to 2 days.

10. About 30 minutes before serving, return the mousse to the food processor and pulse a few times until creamy. Garnish with slices of the remaining banana and the orange zest, and serve.

Tip: Cutting dried fruit is most easily accomplished with kitchen shears or scissors.

Tropical Fruit Tart:

Spread a layer of mousse into a pressed crust (such as the Almond Cookie Crust on page 190). Top with a layer of sliced fresh fruit and toasted coconut. Chill before slicing.

Peanut Butter Mousse
in Chocolate Candy Cups

Yield: 8 to 10 servings (approximately 30 mini cups)
See photo facing page 49.

Peanut Butter Mousse

1 (14- to 16-ounce) package firm tofu (2 cups), blanched (see page 29), and drained

1 cup maple syrup

¾ cup smooth peanut butter, at room temperature

¾ cup light natural cane sugar, or more to taste

¾ cup unsweetened Dutch-process cocoa

1 tablespoon vanilla extract

1 teaspoon almond extract

½ teaspoon salt

I practically lived on peanut butter cup candies one semester at college. I don't know why I was so drawn to them, but I do know it wasn't a good thing. Tofu and organic peanut butter, both healthful foods, are the main players in this more health-ful version of the popular treat, but it's still not okay to eat too many. Of course, if peanut allergies are an issue, you can use another nut butter in its place.

To make the Chocolate Candy Cups, you'll need paper candy cup liners or small cupcake liners (mini cups) and a clean, small watercolor paint brush, small pastry brush, or spoon. A pastry bag will be needed to fill them with the mousse.

1. To prepare the mousse, crumble the tofu into a food processor and process 1 minute. Add the maple syrup and process 1 minute. Add the peanut butter, sugar, cocoa, vanilla and almond extracts, and salt, and process until the mixture is perfectly smooth and creamy. This can take up to 5 minutes. Stop the processor a few times to clean the sides of the bowl.

2. The mousse is ready to use, but can be refrigerated in a covered container for up to two days. Bring to room temperature when ready to use.

Chocolate Candy Cups

8 ounces nondairy
chocolate chips

Tip: Admittedly, this is a
time-consuming process, but
chocolate cups can be frozen
for up to a month in an airtight
container, so make them when
you have time to play.

Chocolate Banana Peanut Butter Cream Parfaits:

If you're short on time, use the
Peanut Butter Mousse in a
parfait. Layer the mousse with
sliced ripe bananas and Ultimate
Chocolate Sauce (page 63) in
parfait dishes, and sprinkle with
peanuts.

3. To prepare the chocolate cups, fit the paper liners into mini muffin tins or place on a baking sheet lined with plastic wrap. Melt the chocolate in a small heatproof bowl placed over a saucepan of barely simmering water. Stir occasionally until the chocolate is melted and smooth. Do not overheat. Remove the bowl from the saucepan.

4. Spoon some melted chocolate into each cup. Use the brush to coat the liners as thoroughly as possible. Make sure to coat the inside rim; you want to prevent it from breaking when the paper is peeled off the chocolate. Wipe off any chocolate that drips onto the outside of the rim. Refrigerate or freeze the cups until the chocolate has hardened; this will take 10 to 30 minutes depending upon how cold your freezer is, and how thick a layer of chocolate you have made. Place the bowl of melted chocolate back on the saucepan and keep it warm over barely simmering water.

5. Check the cups for thin spots. Add another layer of chocolate, coating the thin spots more generously. The chocolate doesn't have to be smooth; the cups will be filled. Chill again until hardened.

6. Slowly and carefully peel the paper off in a spiral motion; don't pull straight down, or the rim may break. (You may find it easier to peel the paper from the cups after you have filled them. Test one or two and decide which method works better for you.)

7. To assemble the candy cups, spoon or pipe some peanut butter cream into each cup using a pastry bag fitted with a plain or star tip. Refrigerate or freeze until ready to serve.

My-T-Satisfying
Chocolate Pudding

Yield: 4 to 6 servings

½ cup light natural cane sugar

6 tablespoons unsweetened Dutch-process cocoa

¼ teaspoon salt

⅓ cup water

2 cups soymilk or soy creamer

2 ounces nondairy semisweet chocolate, broken into small pieces

3 tablespoons cornstarch

1 tablespoon vanilla extract

You may be amazed by how quick and easy it is to make real chocolate pudding from scratch. Both cocoa and chocolate are used to make a pudding that is so satisfying that no one will ever guess it was made without dairy.

1. Combine the sugar, cocoa, and salt in a heavy, medium saucepan. Gradually stir the water into the saucepan and mix to a paste.

2. Bring to a boil over medium heat, stirring frequently. Reduce the heat to low and stir in 1⅔ cups of the soymilk. Simmer for 2 minutes. Add the chocolate and stir gently with a rubber spatula until the chocolate melts.

3. In a small bowl, combine the cornstarch and remaining ⅓ cup of the soymilk, and stir with a fork to dissolve. Add to the simmering chocolate, whisking constantly, and cook, stirring frequently, until the mixture boils. After the pudding has boiled for about 30 seconds, remove from the heat and stir in the vanilla.

4. Pour the pudding into cups or a large bowl. If you'd like to prevent a skin from forming on the pudding, place a piece of waxed paper or parchment paper directly on the pudding while it is hot. Cool and refrigerate for two hours or up to two days.

Tip: Arrowroot can replace the cornstarch, but the texture will be different; arrowroot-based puddings are slightly gooey. Remember to remove arrowroot-thickened foods from the stove as soon as they boil.

Soy-Free Chocolate Pudding:

Substitute rice milk for the soymilk, or for a very lean, but deeply chocolatey pudding, use only water as the liquid. The water variation is the result of a "mistake" made in a chocolate class; we were all surprised at how good the pudding tasted.

Dark Chocolate

Dark chocolate contains several benevolent chemicals. Among them is phenylethylamine, which occurs naturally in the body and is thought to ward off the blues, and stearic acid, which is a unique saturated fat that may lower cholesterol. That's good news, but do base your diet on a variety of whole foods and enjoy eating chocolate as a treat. (I do, nearly every day.) When you eat chocolate, make it high quality, nondairy, naturally sweetened, and organic, and look for fair trade chocolate.

Cocoa beans are one of the most heavily pesticide-laden food crops on the planet. Fair trade is an innovative, market-based approach to sustainable development that helps family farmers in developing countries gain direct access to international markets, as well as develop the business capacity needed to compete in the global marketplace. The result is higher family living standards, thriving communities, and more sustainable farming practices. More information about fair trade is found on page 22.

Creamy Carob Pudding

¼ cup dark whole cane sugar

¼ cup maple syrup

2 teaspoons molasses

¾ cup water

½ cup roasted carob powder

¼ teaspoon salt

1½ cups soymilk or rice milk

2 teaspoons minced orange zest

3 tablespoons cornstarch

1 tablespoon vanilla extract

½ teaspoon orange extract

1 cup Soft Orange Tofu Cream (page 58), for serving

Orange zest, in long thin strips, for garnish

Cooking carob powder in a liquid helps reduce the chalky taste often associated with carob desserts. This cornstarch–based pudding pairs especially well with Soft Orange Tofu Cream.

1. Combine the dark whole cane sugar, maple syrup, and molasses in a heavy, medium saucepan. Stir in ½ cup of the water and bring to a boil over medium heat. Reduce the heat to low and whisk in the carob powder and salt. Cover and simmer, stirring frequently, for 4 to 5 minutes. Stir in the soymilk and zest, and simmer 1 minute longer.

2. Combine the cornstarch with the remaining ¼ cup water in a small bowl and stir with a fork to dissolve. Add to the saucepan, whisking constantly. Cook the mixture about 30 seconds after it boils, whisking constantly. Remove from the heat and add the vanilla and orange extracts. Remove the saucepan from the heat.

3. Pour into serving dishes. Cool to room temperature, cover, and refrigerate about 30 minutes, until set. Serve with a dollop of Soft Orange Tofu Cream and garnish with orange zest.

Tips: Arrowroot can replace the cornstarch, but the texture will be different; arrowroot-based puddings are slightly gooey.

• Remember to remove arrowroot-thickened foods from the stove as soon as they boil.

Coconut Carob Pudding:

Replace the soymilk with unsweetened coconut milk and garnish with toasted coconut.

Softly Gelled Fruit Soup and Blueberry-Fig Salad, p. 40, with Silken Cashew Cream, p. 60

Banana Cream Pudding

Yield: 6 to 8 servings

½ cup dark whole cane sugar

¼ cup cornstarch

¼ teaspoon ground nutmeg

⅛ teaspoon salt

1¾ cups rice milk or soymilk

2 teaspoons vanilla extract

3 ripe bananas

This is essentially a quickly made cornstarch pudding. The key to making great banana pudding is using very ripe bananas, yellow with little brown specks. Bananas ripen best in the dark, so put them in a paper bag and check on them until they're perfect. Anyone who remembers banana pudding made with vanilla wafers will particularly appreciate this recipe. Rice milk will make a lighter colored pudding than soymilk.

1. Combine the dark whole cane sugar, cornstarch, nutmeg, and salt in a medium saucepan, and stir to distribute the ingredients. Add the rice milk slowly, whisking until the mixture is smooth.

2. Bring to a boil over medium heat, stirring frequently. Lower the heat and simmer 1 minute. Remove from the stove and stir in the vanilla.

3. Spoon the pudding into a bowl and cool 10 minutes. Chop 1 of the bananas and fold into the pudding. Serve warm, or cover and refrigerate up to a day ahead. Just before serving, slice the remaining 2 bananas and arrange on top of the pudding.

Banana Cream and Cookie Pudding:

Layer the pudding with Vanilla Wafer Cookies (page 78) in individual dishes.

Chocolate Banana Cream Pudding:

Pour ½ cup of Ultimate Chocolate Sauce (page 63), or more or less to taste, over the bananas.

Peanut Butter Mousse in Chocolate Candy Cups, p. 44

Indian Pudding

Yield: 6 to 8 servings

4 cups soymilk

½ cup fresh yellow cornmeal

¼ cup maple syrup, plus more for serving

3 tablespoons molasses

2 tablespoons maple sugar or dark whole cane sugar

½ teaspoon ground cinnamon

½ teaspoon ground ginger

¼ teaspoon salt

¼ teaspoon ground nutmeg

⅛ teaspoon baking powder

⅛ teaspoon baking soda

⅔ cup pecans, toasted (see page 23), cooled, and coarsely chopped

⅔ cup dried cranberries

Indian pudding is a dish that dates back to the Pilgrims, who referred to cornmeal as Indian meal. This pudding makes a hearty, nutritious breakfast as well as a good ending to a light meal. It is easy to make, but does need a couple hours to bake, so plan ahead. To conserve energy, why not bake a casserole or another dish at the same time?

1. Position a rack in the middle of the oven and preheat to 300 degrees. Oil a 1½- to 2-quart baking dish with canola oil.

2. Pour 1 cup of the soymilk into a small bowl. Add the cornmeal slowly, stirring until no lumps remain.

3. Pour 2¼ cups of the soymilk into a medium saucepan and bring to a boil over medium heat. Lower the heat, and slowly stir in the cornmeal mixture. Simmer, stirring constantly, for 2 or 3 minutes, until the mixture is smooth. Continue to simmer, stirring frequently, for 15 minutes.

4. Remove from the stove and whisk in the maple syrup, molasses, maple sugar, cinnamon, ginger, salt, nutmeg, baking powder, and baking soda.

5. Spoon the pudding into the prepared pan and pour the remaining ¾ cup soymilk over the top. Do not stir the milk into the pudding. Bake for 2 to 2½ hours, until the pudding is almost set. The pudding will be golden brown but the center will still be soft.

6. Cool the pudding on a wire rack for 20 minutes. Serve the pudding warm, sprinkled with the nuts and cranberries, and drizzled with extra maple syrup.

Tip: The pudding can be baked two days ahead. Cool and cover tightly with plastic wrap. To reheat, remove the plastic wrap, cover with parchment, then with aluminum foil, and heat in a 300-degree oven for 20 to 30 minutes.

Gels, Creams, Puddings, Sauces

New Orleans Bread Pudding with Apples and Pecans

Yield: 8 to 10 servings

¾ cup raisins

½ cup orange juice

1 pound dense whole grain bread, thickly sliced (stale is fine)

4 tablespoons arrowroot

2 cups vanilla soymilk

1 cup apple juice

½ cup maple syrup

2 teaspoons ground cinnamon

½ teaspoon ground nutmeg

¼ teaspoon ground cloves

¼ teaspoon salt

2 teaspoons vanilla extract

½ teaspoon almond extract

1 large apple, cored and chopped

¾ cup pecans, toasted (page 23), cooled, and chopped

Tastes Like It Could Be Hard Sauce (page 61)

This is an honest bread pudding made better by eliminating the choles-terol, excess fat, and sugar. Fruit is mixed into this pudding, based on a recipe developed by the late, great chef Frank Acuri, a true Southern gen-tleman. Try some for breakfast.

1. Soak the raisins in ¼ cup of the orange juice for about 10 minutes, until they are plump.

2. Cut the crusts off the bread and cut the bread into 1-inch cubes. Put the bread in a large bowl.

3. Drain the raisins, reserving the orange juice, and add to the bread.

4. Combine the arrowroot and remaining ¼ cup of the orange juice in a medium bowl, and stir with a fork to dissolve. Add the reserved juice, soymilk, apple juice, maple syrup, cinnamon, nutmeg, cloves, salt, and vanilla and almond extracts, and mix until thoroughly combined. Pour over the bread and stir in the chopped apple. Cover the mixture with plastic wrap, and refrigerate for 4 to 8 hours.

5. Before baking, position a rack in the middle of the oven, and preheat to 375 degrees. Oil a 9 x 13-inch baking dish or a 2-quart baking dish with shallow sides.

6. Stir half the pecans into the bread mixture and spoon into the baking dish. Cover the pudding with parchment paper, and overwrap with aluminum foil. Bake for 20 minutes. Remove from the oven, and carefully uncover. Bake 20 minutes longer.

7. Serve the pudding warm or at room temperature with the hard sauce, and sprinkle each serving with some of the remaining nuts. If you prefer, a scoop of a frozen nondairy ice cream melting on top of a bowl of warm pudding is a very good alternative to hard sauce.

Chocolate Cranberry Bread Pudding

Yield: 8 to 10 servings

¾ cup dried cranberries

½ cup orange juice

1 pound dense whole grain bread, thickly sliced (stale is fine)

4 tablespoons arrowroot

2 cups chocolate soymilk

1 cup apple juice

¼ cup maple syrup

2 teaspoons ground cinnamon

½ teaspoon ground nutmeg

¼ teaspoon ground cloves

¼ teaspoon salt

2 teaspoons vanilla extract

½ teaspoon almond extract

2 ripe bananas, sliced thick

6 ounces nondairy semisweet chocolate, cut into chunks (1 cup)

¾ cup pecans, toasted (see page 23), cooled, and chopped

Utimate Chocolate Sauce (page 63)

This bread pudding is definitely a dessert rather than a breakfast dish.

1. Soak the cranberries in ¼ cup of the orange juice for about 10 minutes, until they are plump.

2. Cut the crusts off the bread and cut the bread into 1-inch cubes. Put the bread in a large bowl.

3. Drain the cranberries, reserving the orange juice, and add to the bread.

4. Combine the arrowroot and remaining ¼ cup of orange juice in a medium bowl, and stir with a fork to dissolve. Add the reserved juice, soymilk, apple juice, maple syrup, cinnamon, nutmeg, cloves, salt, and vanilla and almond extracts, and mix until thoroughly combined. Pour over the bread and stir in the bananas. Cover the mixture with plastic wrap, and refrigerate for 4 to 8 hours.

5. Before baking, position a rack in the middle of the oven, and preheat to 375 degrees. Oil a 9 x 13-inch baking dish or a 2-quart baking dish with shallow sides.

6. Stir the chocolate chunks and half the pecans into the bread mixture and spoon into the baking dish. Cover the pudding with parchment paper, and overwrap with aluminum foil. Bake for 20 minutes. Remove from the oven, and carefully remove the foil. Bake 20 minutes longer.

7. Serve the pudding warm or at room temperature with the chocolate sauce, and sprinkle each serving with some of the remaining nuts.

Gels, Creams, Puddings, Sauces

Maple Brown Rice and Raisin Pudding

Yield: 6 to 8 servings

2 cups cooked brown rice (recipe page 55)

1 cup rice milk or soymilk

2/3 cup raisins

1 (12.3-ounce) box firm silken tofu (1 1/3 cups)

1/3 cup brown rice syrup

1/4 cup maple syrup, plus more for serving

1 tablespoon arrowroot

1 tablespoon vanilla extract

1 1/2 teaspoons ground cinnamon

1/2 teaspoon ground nutmeg

3 tablespoons maple sugar or light natural cane sugar

A great–tasting comfort food packed with nutritious ingredients, rice pudding makes a nourishing breakfast as well as a sensible end to a light meal. Cook extra rice and keep it refrigerated for up to three days in a covered container for rice pudding in a flash. A spoonful of Ginger Tofu Whip (page 57) is a nice complement to this pudding.

1. Position a rack in the middle of the oven and preheat to 375 degrees. Oil a 1 1/2-quart baking dish.

2. Put the rice in a food processor and pulse two or three times. Add the rice milk and pulse until the rice mixture is creamy but not perfectly smooth (some of the texture of the rice should remain). Pour the rice mixture into a large bowl. (Don't wash the food processor bowl). Stir in the raisins.

3. Add the tofu, rice syrup, maple syrup, arrowroot, vanilla, 1/2 teaspoon of the cinnamon, and the nutmeg to the food processor, and process until smooth. Pour into the puréed rice, and mix until combined.

4. Cover the pudding with a piece of parchment paper, and overwrap with aluminum foil. Bake for 25 minutes. Uncover and bake for 10 or 15 minutes longer, or until the pudding is bubbling. Remove the pudding from the oven, and cool on a wire rack for 15 minutes. The pudding firms as it cools.

5. Mix the sugar and the remaining 1 teaspoon cinnamon in a small bowl, and sprinkle over the pudding. Serve warm or at room temperature, drizzled with more maple syrup.

Spiced Pumpkin Rice Pudding

Yield: 6 to 8 servings

2 cups cooked brown rice (page 55)

3 cups soymilk

¼ cup dark whole cane sugar

1 teaspoon ground cinnamon

½ teaspoon ground nutmeg

Dash salt

2 cups Spiced Pumpkin Purée (page 55) or 1 (15-ounce) can pumpkin purée

⅔ cup dried cranberries or raisins

½ cup toasted pecans, chopped (see page 23)

The lovely orange hue, spicy scent, and terrific taste make this unusual pudding a winner.

1. Combine the rice, soymilk, dark whole cane sugar, cinnamon, nutmeg, and salt in a 2-quart ovenproof baking dish with a lid. Bring to a boil over medium heat, stirring a few times. Reduce the heat, cover, and simmer for 20 minutes.

2. Position a rack in the middle of the oven and preheat to 375 degrees.

3. Uncover and place the baking dish in the oven. Bake for 15 minutes, stirring twice. Remove the baking dish from the oven and reduce the temperature to 350 degrees. Stir in the Spiced Pumpkin Purée. Cover and bake 15 minutes longer.

4. Cool the baking dish on a wire rack for about 10 minutes. Sprinkle the pudding with the cranberries and pecans, and serve warm.

Basic Brown Rice

Yield: 2 cups cooked rice

1 cup medium-grain brown rice

2 cups water

½ teaspoon salt, or more to taste

Brown rice is rich in fiber, trace minerals, and B vitamins. Cook extra rice to have on hand for soups, salads, cereals, and desserts. Refrigerate in an airtight container for up to three days.

1. Rinse the rice in a bowl of water. Drain.

2. Place the water and salt in a medium saucepan and bring to a boil over high heat. Stir in the rice and return to a boil. Reduce the heat to very low, cover, and simmer for 45 to 55 minutes, until the rice is tender. Remove from the heat and let the rice stand, covered, for 10 minutes.

Spiced Pumpkin Purée

Yield: 2 cups

2 cups (16 ounces) unsweetened pumpkin purée

2/3 cup dark whole cane sugar

1½ teaspoons ground cinnamon

1 teaspoon ground ginger

½ teaspoon salt

½ teaspoon ground nutmeg

¼ teaspoon ground cloves

This purée can be cooked up to two days ahead and refrigerated in an airtight container, but use it at room temperature. While you are cooking, why not make a double recipe? Freeze the extra in an airtight container for up to one month. Defrost and use the purée to make Spiced Pumpkin Cranberry Muffins (page 118) and Pumpkin Pecan Bread (page 120).

1. Combine all the ingredients in a medium saucepan. Cook over low heat, stirring frequently, until the mixture comes to a simmer and sputters. Simmer for 3 to 4 minutes, stirring constantly until the purée is dark, shiny, and thickened, and the sugar has dissolved.

2. Remove from the heat and spoon into a container. Cool, cover, and refrigerate or freeze. Allow time for the purée to return to room temperature before using.

Terrific Maple Tofu Whip

1 cup firm tofu (half a 14- to 16-ounce package), blanched (see page 29) and drained

1 tablespoon plus 1 teaspoon canola oil

5 tablespoons maple syrup

2 tablespoons light natural cane sugar, or more for a sweeter whip

2 teaspoons fresh lemon juice

2 teaspoons vanilla extract

¼ teaspoon salt

⅛ teaspoon ground cinnamon

This cream has body and great taste. It is easily doubled and will complement many desserts.

1. Crumble the tofu into a blender or food processor and process for 1 minute. Add the rest of the ingredients and process until the mixture is very smooth. This will take about 5 minutes. Stop the blender or processor a few times and clean the sides of the jar or bowl with a rubber spatula. Taste and add more sugar if you want a sweeter whip.

2. Spoon the cream into a container. Cover and refrigerate for 3 hours or longer to allow the flavors to blend. The cream will become slightly thicker as it chills. Store in a covered container in the refrigerator for up to two days.

Ginger Tofu Whip

1 cup firm tofu (half a 14- to 16-ounce package), blanched (see page 29) and drained

1 tablespoon plus 1 teaspoon canola oil

¼ cup maple syrup

2 tablespoons dark whole cane sugar

2 tablespoons light natural cane sugar, or more to taste

1 tablespoon fresh ginger juice

1 tablespoon frozen orange juice concentrate

2 teaspoons vanilla extract

½ teaspoon ground ginger dissolved in 1 teaspoon water

¼ teaspoon orange extract

¼ teaspoon salt

¼ teaspoon ground nutmeg

Both ground ginger and fresh ginger juice flavor this unusual, spicy tofu whip. Ginger pairs exceptionally well with fruit–flavored desserts, especially those that contain apples, pears, or oranges.

1. Crumble the tofu into a blender or food processor and process for 1 minute. Add the rest of the ingredients. Process until the mixture is very smooth; this will take about 5 minutes. Stop the blender or processor a few times and clean the sides of the jar or bowl with a rubber spatula. Taste and add more sugar if you want a sweeter whip.

2. Spoon the cream into a container. Cover and refrigerate for at least 3 hours to allow the flavors to blend. The cream will become slightly thicker as it chills. Refrigerate this tofu cream for up to three days.

Soft Orange Tofu Cream

Yield: 1³/₄ cups

1 (12.3-ounce) box firm
    or extra-firm silken
    tofu (1⅓ cups),
    drained (see page 29)

5 tablespoons light
    natural cane sugar,
    or more to taste

5 tablespoons orange
    juice concentrate,
    thawed

1 tablespoon canola
    oil

2 teaspoons vanilla
    extract

¼ teaspoon orange
    extract

Transform simple fruit salads into special treats, amp up plain cakes, and complement kantens, cobblers, and more with a dollop of this versatile cream. Silken tofu is used straight from the package and makes cream that is softer than those made with regular tofu.

1. Combine all the ingredients in a blender or food processor, and process 2 to 3 minutes, or until thoroughly mixed and creamy. Taste the cream and add more sugar if you want a sweeter whip.

2. Spoon the cream into a container. Cover and refrigerate for at least 3 hours to allow the flavors to blend. The cream will thicken slightly when chilled. Refrigerate for up to two days.

Strawberry Tofu Cream

Yield: 2 cups

1 (12.3-ounce) box firm or extra-firm silken tofu (1⅓ cups), drained (see page 29)

⅓ cup all-fruit strawberry jam, or more to taste

¾ cup light natural cane sugar, or more to taste

1 tablespoon plus 1 teaspoon fresh lemon juice

1 teaspoon minced lemon zest

1 teaspoon vanilla extract

½ teaspoon salt

Like the preceding orange cream, this tofu cream is made with silken tofu. If you like strawberry shortcake, fold sliced, sugared strawberries into this cream, pair with the biscuits on page 110, and you'll be serving shortcakes.

1. Combine all the ingredients in a blender or food processor, and process 2 to 3 minutes, or until thoroughly mixed and creamy. Taste the cream and add more sugar or jam if you want a sweeter whip.

2. Spoon the cream into a container. Cover and refrigerate for at least 3 hours to allow the flavors to blend. The cream will thicken slightly when chilled. Refrigerate for up to two days.

Silken Cashew Cream

Yield: 1½ cups

1 cup raw cashews

½ cup brown
  rice syrup

¼ cup water

¼ teaspoon salt

1 tablespoon vanilla
  extract

¼ teaspoon almond
  extract

Tip: Store a container of Silken Cashew Cream in your freezer. It will keep for up to one month and defrosts quickly.

Rich in taste and texture only, this indispensable nut cream, gently sweetened with brown rice syrup, transforms simple fruits into stylish treats and enlivens puddings, shortcakes, and many other desserts.

1. Position a rack in the middle of the oven and preheat to 300 degrees. Line a baking sheet with parchment paper. Spread the cashews on the sheet and toast in the oven for 4 or 5 minutes, until fragrant but not colored. Cool completely.

2. The rice syrup will be easier to measure if warmed first. Place the jar of syrup in a saucepan and fill the saucepan halfway up the jar with water. Bring to a simmer over low heat. Stir the syrup once or twice until it has liquefied.

3. Grind the cashews into a fine meal in a food processor. Add the rice syrup and process until the mixture is smooth, stopping the processor a few times to scrape down the sides of the work bowl. Add the water, salt, and vanilla and almond extracts, and process until completely smooth, 3 to 5 minutes or longer.

4. Store in a covered container in the refrigerator for up to two weeks. The cream will thicken more when cold; thin with water if desired and stir before serving.

Other Nut Creams:

Cashews make the richest, smoothest nut cream, but other roasted nuts, including blanched almonds, skinned hazelnuts, and pecans, create flavorful creams. The exception is walnuts, which are too bitter for this recipe.

Gels, Creams, Puddings, Sauces

Tastes Like It Could Be Hard Sauce

Yield: 2 cups

2 cups apple or pear juice

½ cup soymilk

1 to 2 tablespoons mirin (see note below) or whiskey

2 tablespoons arrowroot

2 tablespoons orange juice

2 teaspoons vanilla extract

1 teaspoon almond extract

½ teaspoon orange extract

Tip: Pour some Tastes Like It Could Be Hard Sauce on rice pudding, chocolate and carob puddings, biscuits —and more.

But it's not. Hard sauce, also called whiskey sauce, is a popular accompaniment to bread pudding in the southern United States. Typical recipes call for one stick of butter, two eggs, one cup of whiskey, and a lot of sugar, but this better–for–you version got raves from a couple of Southern tasters.

1. Bring the juice to a boil over medium heat in a small saucepan. Continue to boil until it has reduced to 1 cup. Lower the heat and stir in the soymilk and mirin. (If you are using whiskey, wait to add it at the end of step 2.) Simmer 2 to 3 minutes.

2. In a small bowl, combine the arrowroot and orange juice, and stir with a fork to dissolve. Add the dissolved arrowroot to the juice mixture, whisking constantly. Cook over medium heat only until the liquid boils. Immediately remove the saucepan from the heat, and stir in the vanilla, almond, and orange extracts. (If you cook or stir arrowroot-thickened mixtures after they have boiled, they are likely to become thin again.) If you are using the whiskey, add it now.

Mirin

Mirin is a sweet, low-alcohol, golden wine that adds sweetness and flavor to a variety of dishes, sauces, and glazes. Made from glutinous rice, it's available in Japanese markets and the gourmet section of many supermarkets. Mirin is also referred to simply as rice wine.

Maple Cider Syrup

1 cup plus 1 tablespoon apple cider

4 tablespoons maple syrup

½ teaspoon ground cinnamon

4 teaspoons arrowroot

1 teaspoon vanilla extract

Minced orange zest (optional)

Tip: Raisins and nuts are nice additions to the sauce.

Good with pancakes, fruit, and bread and rice puddings, this is a less sweet, less expensive alternative to maple syrup. Serve the syrup warm.

1. Combine 1 cup of the apple cider, the maple syrup, and cinnamon in a small saucepan and bring to a boil over medium heat. Reduce the heat to low and simmer for 10 minutes.

2. In a small bowl, combine the arrowroot and the remaining tablespoon cider, and stir with a fork to dissolve. Add the dissolved arrowroot to the simmering cider, whisking constantly. Cook over medium heat only until the liquid boils. Immediately remove the saucepan from the heat, and stir in the vanilla and zest. (If you cook or stir arrowroot-thickened mixtures after they have boiled, they are likely to become thin again.) Cool and refrigerate in a covered container for up to three days.

Ultimate Chocolate Sauce

Yield: 1½ cups

½ cup water

¾ cup unsweetened Dutch-process cocoa

½ cup light natural cane sugar

¼ teaspoon salt

½ cup maple syrup

2 tablespoons canola oil

1 tablespoon vanilla extract

Tip: The sauce will thicken slightly after chilling in the refrigerator; allow time for the sauce to return to room temperature if you are making Ultimate Chocolate Icing (page 147).

Keep a jar of this versatile, delicious, and virtually fat–free sauce in your refrigerator; I am sure you will think of many ways to use it. I like to drizzle a few spoonfuls over puddings, cakes, and nondairy desserts (eating it directly off a spoon is an option!). This recipe is used to make Ultimate Chocolate Icing (page 148).

1. Pour the water into a small saucepan and bring to a boil. Remove from the heat.

2. Combine the cocoa, sugar, and salt in the bowl of a blender or food processor. Pulse a few times to mix. With the motor running, pour 6 tablespoons of the hot water through the feed tube. Stop the blender or food processor, and clean the sides with a rubber spatula. Add the maple syrup, oil, and vanilla. Process about 1 minute, until smooth. The sauce will be thin.

3. Pour the sauce into a jar with a lid. Refrigerate the sauce for up to one week, or freeze for up to one month.

Raspberry Coulis

4 cups fresh or frozen raspberries, very slightly defrosted

⅓ to 1 cup light natural cane sugar, finely ground in a blender (see tips)

1 tablespoon fresh lemon juice

1 teaspoon minced lemon zest (optional)

Tips: Taste a few berries before you proceed to determine if the coulis will need more or less sugar.

• Because light natural cane sugar is coarser than superfine sugar, the type of sugar typically used to make berry sauces, it must be ground in a blender for a minute or two until fine.

Versatile and quickly made berry sauces (also known as coulis) complement gels, puddings, frozen desserts, cakes, and more. Fresh seasonal berries are always the best choice, but frozen, unsweetened organic berries work nicely too.

1. Purée the berries with ⅓ cup sugar and the lemon juice in a blender or food processor. Continue to process until the sugar is completely dissolved; this could take 2 to 3 minutes.

2. Taste and add additional sweetener, if needed, a little at a time. Process after each addition of sugar until the sugar is dissolved. Rub a bit of purée in your fingers; it should not be gritty.

3. Place a fine mesh sieve over a bowl. Pour the purée into the sieve and push hard on the solids to strain it. Stir the lemon zest, if using, into the strained mixture.

4. Refrigerate the coulis in a covered container for up to one day.

Berry Coulis:

Replace the raspberries with an equal amount of fresh or frozen strawberries, blueberries, or other berries of your choice.

How to Choose, Wash, and Store Fresh Raspberries

Raspberries are generally available from midsummer through early fall. Fragrantly sweet with a subtly tart overtone, raspberries are delicious and are usually in limited supply, but organic frozen raspberries are readily available. Raspberries are highly perishable and should not be purchased more than one or two days prior to use. Choose firm, plump, deeply colored berries. If you are buying berries prepackaged in a container, make sure the container shows no signs of stains or moisture, indications of possible spoilage. Before putting the berries in the refrigerator, remove any berries that are mushy or moldy. Line the original container with a piece of paper towel and return the berries to the container.

Wash the berries very gently, just before they will be eaten or prepared. Use the light pressure of the sink sprayer, if possible, and gently pat them dry.

Raspberries are very low in calories and contain nutritious amounts of vitamin C and manganese, plus fiber. Red raspberries are most often the source of a dietary supplement called ellagic acid, a phenolic compound thought to have anticancer properties.

Chapter 3... Great Good Cookies, Bars, and Little Bites

Introducing Great Good Cookies, Bars, and Bites Naturally

Crisp cookies, soft cookies, thin cookies, bars, and little bites—the aroma of fresh baked cookies is surely one of life's nicest small pleasures. They are one of the most popular comfort foods, and everyone has a favorite! Cookies are easily made from only a few ingredients; the most difficult part of preparing them may be trying not to eat too many. The word "cookie" comes from the Dutch word koekje, which means little cake. In fact, bar cookies, such as brownies, are made from a cake-like batter.

The Secrets to Making Nondairy Cookies and Bars

- Think like a pastry chef and get organized before you start. Read the recipe carefully, all the way through.

- Use good-quality ingredients and make sure everything you need is at hand and prepped as needed (toast and cool nuts, seeds, or coconut; melt chocolate). Review A Baker's Dozen Secrets to Successful Desserts (page 32).

- Use the appropriate measuring cups: nested, straight-sided cups for dry ingredients and glass or plastic cups with pouring spouts for liquid ones.

- Preheat the oven and line the baking sheets with parchment paper. When you are baking two sheets of cookies together, position one rack in the middle of the oven and the second one above it. Use the middle rack to bake a single sheet.

- Cookie dough generally contains less liquid than cake batters, and cookies are formed individually. The batter is dropped from a spoon, shaped by hand, or rolled and stamped out with cookie cutters.

- Feel free to change the size of the cookies, but shape them uniformly, so they bake evenly.

- Make a variety of cookies from a single recipe. For example, roll the dough in chopped nuts or toasted coconut before baking, or stir chips, nuts, and seeds into the batter. Sandwich two baked cookies together with a filling of jam, melted chocolate, or icing, or dip one end of a cookie into melted chocolate, then dip the chocolate into finely ground nuts or toasted coconut.

- Cookies are often baked in several batches. Allow the baking sheets to cool between batches.

- Cookies bake in a relatively short time. Use a timer and don't overbake them. Turn the baking sheet front to back halfway through baking.

- Remove the baking sheets from the oven and place directly on wire racks. Don't try to move the cookies until they are firm enough to release from the parchment paper unless the recipe says otherwise.

- Most of the cookies in this book are relatively low in fat and taste best eaten within two days, unless the recipe indicates otherwise. (Lower-fat baked goods become stale quickly.) Cookies and bars freeze well. Place them in airtight containers (or zipper-lock bags with the air pressed out) in the freezer for one month.

- Store soft cookies in plastic containers or zipper-lock plastic bags, and keep crisp cookies in tins or tightly covered jars.

Baking Sheet, Cookie Sheet, Baking Pan, Sheet Pan, Jelly Roll Pan: What's the Difference?

- A pan that is rimless on at least one side is called a cookie sheet. A pan with shallow rims on all four sides is known variously as a baking sheet, sheet pan, or jelly roll pan. I suggest you buy a few heavy baking sheets in the largest size that will fit into your oven and use them to bake cookies and thin sheet cakes, to keep nuts, seeds, oats, and granola from spilling during handling, and to contain spillover from juicy fruit pies. Heavy baking sheets will not warp or bend in a hot oven.

- I use baking sheets as my primary cookie sheets. Cookies bake most evenly on shiny, light-colored aluminum baking sheets. Lining the sheet with parchment paper protects the dough from the aluminum and creates a nonstick surface. Don't bake cookies on dark-colored baking sheets, as they will often become too brown, if not burnt. Reserve dark sheets for pies, which need strong bottom heat to set the crust.

Crisp and Chewy Lace Cookies (Wheat Free)

Yield: about 18 (3^1/$_2$-inch) cookies

½ cup rolled oats

½ cup whole raw almonds

½ cup rice flour

½ teaspoon ground cinnamon

½ teaspoon plus ¼ teaspoon baking powder

¼ teaspoon ground nutmeg

⅛ teaspoon salt

1 tablespoon plus 1½ teaspoons canola oil

2 tablespoons plus 1½ teaspoons maple syrup

2 tablespoons brown rice syrup

1 teaspoon vanilla extract

½ teaspoon almond extract

This recipe, to be honest, resulted from a mistake in measuring. During a recipe testing session, my assistant Kevin noticed the cookies had spread too much—they looked terrible. To our amazement, less than five minutes out of the oven the cookies set and became ultra–thin, lacy, chewy–crisp sensations. Sometimes you get lucky, and we were lucky that morning.

1. Position a rack in the middle of the oven and another rack above it, and preheat to 325 degrees. Line two baking sheets with parchment paper.

2. Grind the oats in a blender or food processor until fine. Add the almonds and process until the mixture resembles coarse meal. Pour into a medium bowl, and add the rice flour, cinnamon, baking powder, nutmeg, and salt. Stir to distribute the ingredients.

3. Whisk the oil, maple syrup, rice syrup, and vanilla and almond extracts in a small bowl until well blended. Pour into the dry mixture and stir with a rubber spatula until a piece of dough holds together when squeezed. The dough will be sticky.

4. Shape the dough into 1-inch balls, and place them 4 inches apart on the prepared sheets. If you have to bake the cookies in batches, remember to allow the sheets to cool in between.

5. Bake for 8 to 9 minutes, or until the cookies have spread and are no longer bubbling.

6. Set the baking sheet on a rack and cool about 5 minutes. Slide the cookies, still on the parchment paper, onto a rack and cool completely. Keep the cookies in a covered jar or tin for two days.

Famous Jam Dots

Yield: 2 dozen (1-inch) cookies

1 cup rolled oats

1 cup pecans

1¼ cups whole wheat pastry flour

¼ teaspoon baking powder

¼ teaspoon ground cinnamon

¼ teaspoon ground nutmeg

⅛ teaspoon salt

½ cup canola oil

½ cup maple syrup

1 teaspoon vanilla extract

½ teaspoon almond extract

⅓ cup all-fruit jam (any flavor)

Tip: Fill some of the cookies with either raspberry or apricot jam.

Chocolate Dot Cookies:

Fill the centers with a few nondairy chocolate chips.

Here is my slightly tweaked version of the Natural Gourmet Institute of Food and Health's popular Jam Dot Cookies, with thanks to the school director, Jennie Matthau. Rumor has it that many visitors enroll for a class at the Institute after a taste of this cookie.

1. Position a rack in the middle of the oven and another rack above it. Preheat to 325 degrees. Line two baking sheets with parchment paper.

2. Spread the oats on one of the prepared sheets and the pecans on the other. Toast each pan in the oven for 6 minutes. Cool completely, leaving the parchment on the sheets for baking the cookies. Raise the oven temperature to 350 degrees.

3. Put the oats in a blender or food processor, and process until fine. Add the pecans and process until the mixture resembles coarse meal. Pour into a medium bowl and add the pastry flour, baking powder, cinnamon, nutmeg, and salt.

4. Whisk the oil, maple syrup, and vanilla and almond extracts in a small bowl until well blended. Pour into the dry mixture and stir with a rubber spatula until the dough holds together when squeezed.

5. Shape the dough into 1-inch balls and place 1 inch apart on the prepared sheets. Use your little finger to make an indentation in the center of each cookie. Spoon ½ teaspoon jam in each indentation.

6. Bake for 15 to 16 minutes, or until the cookies are light brown on the bottom.

7. Set the baking sheets on racks and cool for 3 minutes, until the cookies are firm enough to move. Transfer the cookies to a rack to cool. Keep the cookies at room temperature in a covered container or a zipper-lock plastic bag for two days.

Orange Ginger Crisps

Yield: about 3 dozen (2-inch) cookies

See photo facing page 97.

¼ cup whole wheat pastry flour

¼ cup unbleached white flour

2 tablespoons arrowroot

2 teaspoons ground ginger

¼ teaspoon salt

Dash ground mustard (optional)

¼ cup brown rice syrup (see tip)

¼ cup maple syrup

2 tablespoons canola oil

2 tablespoons orange juice

1 teaspoon orange extract

¼ teaspoon vanilla extract

These thin, crisp cookies are quite pungent. If you prefer a milder taste, reduce the ground ginger to 3/4 teaspoon. It's best to bake these cookies one sheet at a time, as they bake more easily in the middle of the oven and must be shaped while still warm. The batter can be refrigerated for eight to twelve hours.

1. Position a rack in the middle of the oven and preheat to 325 degrees. Line two baking sheets with parchment paper.

2. Place a wire mesh strainer over a medium bowl. Add the pastry flour, white flour, arrowroot, ginger, salt, and ground mustard, if using, to the strainer. Tap the strainer against the palm of your hand to sift the ingredients into the bowl. Stir with a wire whisk to distribute the ingredients.

3. Whisk the rice syrup, maple syrup, oil, orange juice, and orange and vanilla extracts in a small bowl until well blended. Pour into the dry mixture and mix until the batter is smooth. The consistency will be similar to pancake batter and should drop off a spoon into a round shape. (If too thin, refrigerate the batter for 20 to 30 minutes until it has thickened.)

4. Use a teaspoon to drop rounds of batter gently, neatly, and uniformly 2 inches apart on the prepared sheet. These cookies spread quite a bit.

5. Bake one sheet at a time for 13 to 15 minutes, until the edges are lightly browned.

6. Allow the cookies to rest on the sheet for 1 minute. Slide the cookies, still on the parchment paper, off the sheet onto a rack. Cool for 10 minutes, until the cookies release easily. Store in an airtight tin at room temperature for up to four days.

Tip: The rice syrup will be easier to measure if warmed first. Place the jar of syrup in a saucepan and fill halfway up the jar with water. Bring to a simmer over low heat. Stir the syrup once or twice until it has liquefied.

Tuiles:

Increase the amount of batter per cookie to 1 tablespoon each. As soon as the cookies are removed from the oven, working one cookie at a time, slide a thin metal spatula under each. Press onto a narrow, round utensil, such as a rolling pin or jar turned on its side. The cookies will set almost instantly. (The cookies must be warm in order to be shaped. Warm the cookies in a 250-degree oven for a few minutes if they harden before all are shaped.)

Cookie Cups:

Increase the amount of batter per cookie to 1 tablespoon each. As soon as the cookies are removed from the oven, working one cookie at a time, slide a thin metal spatula under each. Drape a warm cookie over the bottom of a small cup or jar. The cookies will set almost instantly. (The cookies must be warm in order to be shaped. Warm the cookies in a 250-degree oven for a few minutes if they harden before all are shaped.) Fill the cookie cups with pudding, mousse, or a small scoop of nondairy frozen dessert.

Oatmeal Raisin Cookies

Yield: about 16 (2-inch) cookies

¼ cup raisins

¼ cup orange or apple juice

1 cup rolled oats

¾ cup whole wheat pastry flour

½ cup oat flour (see page 75)

1 teaspoon ground cinnamon

½ teaspoon salt

¼ teaspoon baking powder

¼ teaspoon baking soda

⅓ cup maple syrup

2 tablespoons plus 1 teaspoon canola oil

1 tablespoon molasses or barley malt

1 tablespoon vanilla extract

1 teaspoon apple cider vinegar

We can't have a cookie chapter without oatmeal raisin cookies, but we can make them without butter, eggs, and refined sugar.

1. Position a rack in the middle of the oven and another rack above it. Preheat to 350 degrees. Line two baking sheets with parchment paper.

2. Soak the raisins in the juice for about 10 minutes, until they are plump. Drain the raisins, reserving the juice.

3. Combine the oats, pastry flour, oat flour, cinnamon, salt, baking powder, and baking soda in a medium bowl, and stir to distribute the ingredients.

4. In a separate bowl, whisk 1 tablespoon of the reserved juice, the maple syrup, oil, molasses, vanilla, and vinegar until well blended. Pour into the dry mixture and mix until a piece of dough holds together when squeezed. Add more orange juice, a teaspoon at a time, if needed to make the dough moister. Stir the raisins into the dough.

5. Shape the dough into 1-inch balls, place 1 inch apart on the prepared baking sheets, and flatten slightly with your palm.

6. Bake for 7 to 8 minutes, or until slightly puffed and set. Check the bottom of one cookie; it should be lightly browned.

7. Allow the cookies to rest on the sheets for 1 minute. With a spatula, transfer the cookies to a rack to cool. Store in plastic containers or zipper-lock plastic bags for up to three days.

Oatmeal Chip Cookies:

Omit the raisins and stir ¼ cup nondairy chocolate chips into the batter.

Nutty Oatmeal Raisin Cookies:

Add ½ teaspoon almond extract and ¼ cup chopped nuts to the batter.

Make Your Own Oat Flour

Oat flour is available in natural food stores and some supermarkets, but if you just have rolled oats on hand, you can grind oats into flour in a blender or food processor, a few cups at a time. To make 1 cup of oat flour, start with 1¼ cups rolled oats. You may have a little extra oat flour; it's difficult to be precise. Store the flour in a zipper-lock plastic bag or tightly closed container in the freezer for up to two months.

Oat Sesame Squares (Wheat Free)

Yield: 16 to 20 (1-inch) squares

½ cup sesame seeds

2 cups oat flour (see page 75)

½ teaspoon ground cinnamon

¼ teaspoon salt

4 tablespoons canola oil

5 tablespoons maple syrup

1 teaspoon vanilla extract

½ teaspoon almond extract

Crunchy with calcium–rich sesame seeds, this cookie dough makes a delicious pressed 9–inch tart dough too.

1. Toast the sesame seeds in a dry skillet over low heat for 3 to 4 minutes, stirring constantly. Cool completely.

2. Combine the oat flour, cinnamon, and salt in a medium bowl. Add the sesame seeds and stir to mix.

3. Combine the oil, maple syrup, and vanilla and almond extracts in a small bowl, and whisk until well blended. Pour into the oat mixture and stir with a spatula until the dough holds together when squeezed. Cover the bowl and refrigerate the dough for 15 minutes.

4. Position a rack in the middle of the oven and preheat to 350 degrees. Line a baking sheet with parchment paper.

5. Remove the dough from the refrigerator and place between two 9 x 13-inch pieces of parchment paper. Pound the dough with a rolling pin a few times. Roll the dough to a rough rectangle, ¼ to ½ inch thick.

6. Remove the top piece of parchment paper. Lift the dough, still on the bottom sheet of parchment paper, onto a baking sheet. Press the dough as necessary to smooth any cracks. Trim the outer edges of the dough to make straight sides, saving the scraps to bake as sample pieces. Cut the dough into 16 to 20 squares. Bake for 9 to 11 minutes, until the squares are very lightly brown, and remove from the oven.

7. Place the sheet on a rack for 5 minutes. Slide the squares, still on the parchment paper, onto the rack and cool. Separate the squares and store in an airtight tin or jar at room temperature for up to three days.

Chocolate Chip Cookies

7 tablespoons light natural cane sugar plus ¼ cup for shaping

¼ cup whole wheat pastry flour

¼ cup unbleached white flour

2 tablespoons arrowroot

1 tablespoon dark whole cane sugar

1 tablespoon unsweetened Dutch-process cocoa

½ teaspoon ground cinnamon

¼ teaspoon salt

¼ teaspoon baking powder

⅛ teaspoon baking soda

1 tablespoon plus 2 teaspoons canola oil

2 tablespoons maple syrup

1 tablespoon soymilk

2 teaspoons vanilla extract

½ teaspoon almond extract

Heaping ⅓ cup nondairy chocolate chips

These are thin, chewy cookies that are especially delicious eaten warm from the oven. They become crisp when cool.

1. Position a rack in the middle of the oven and preheat to 350 degrees. Line two baking sheets with parchment paper.

2. Place a wire mesh strainer over a medium bowl. Add 7 tablespoons of the sugar, the pastry flour, white flour, arrowroot, dark whole cane sugar, cocoa, cinnamon, salt, baking powder, and baking soda to the strainer. Tap the strainer against the palm of your hand to sift the ingredients into the bowl. Stir with a wire whisk to distribute the ingredients.

3. Whisk the oil, maple syrup, soymilk, and vanilla and almond extracts in a separate bowl until thoroughly combined. Pour into the dry mixture and mix only until smooth. Add the chips and use your hands to work them into the dough.

4. Sprinkle a piece of plastic wrap with 2 tablespoons of the sugar. Turn the dough out of the bowl onto the sugar. With the aid of the wrap, shape the dough into a log. If the dough is too soft, refrigerate it for about 30 minutes or until it is firm enough to shape.

5. To shape the cookies, spread the remaining 2 tablespoons sugar on a plate. Unwrap the dough and shape into 1-inch balls. Roll the balls in the sugar, and flatten slightly. Place the cookies 3 inches apart on the prepared baking sheets; they spread a great deal.

6. Bake the cookies, one sheet at a time, for 7 to 8 minutes. The cookies will look soft but set.

7. Set the baking sheet on a rack and cool for 3 minutes, until the cookies are firm enough to move. Transfer the cookies to a rack to cool. Store the cookies in a tightly covered tin or jar at room temperature for one to two days.

Vanilla Wafer Cookies

Yield: 2½ dozen (2-inch) cookies

See photo facing page 97.

¾ cup unbleached white flour

¼ cup arrowroot

½ teaspoon baking powder

⅛ teaspoon salt

3 tablespoons canola oil

3 tablespoons maple syrup

2 tablespoons vanilla extract

½ cup light natural cane sugar for sprinkling, more if needed

Several tasters said these cookies reminded them of animal crackers or plain arrowroot cookies. The dough is quite versatile and can be used to make several types of cookies; my favorite variations follow the recipe.

1. Place a wire mesh strainer over a medium bowl. Add the flour, arrowroot, baking powder, and salt to the strainer. Tap the strainer against the palm of your hand to sift the ingredients into the bowl. Stir with a wire whisk to distribute the ingredients.

2. Whisk the oil, maple syrup, and vanilla in a small bowl until well combined. Pour into the dry mixture and mix with a rubber spatula until the dough is smooth and shiny; it will be soft.

3. Divide the dough in half, pat each half into a flat disk and wrap each disk in plastic wrap. Refrigerate 1 hour, until the dough is cold enough to roll and cut.

4. Position a rack in the middle of the oven and preheat to 350 degrees. Line two baking sheets with parchment paper. Spread ½ cup of the sugar on one of the sheets.

5. Remove one piece of dough from the refrigerator and unwrap it onto a piece of parchment paper. Cover with another piece of parchment paper and roll the dough with a rolling pin into a round or oval shape, about ¼ inch thick. Press a cookie cutter into the

dough, making the cuts as close together as possible. Lift the dough remnants from between the cookies; press together, roll out, and cut more cookies. Lightly press the cookies in the sugar and sprinkle the tops of the cookies with sugar as well.

6. Carefully lift the cookies, using a wide spatula, onto the prepared baking sheet, placing them ½ inch apart. If the cookies have become too soft to move to the baking sheet, refrigerate for about 15 minutes until chilled and firm.

7. Bake for 8 to 10 minutes, or until the cookies look dry and slightly puffed and the bottoms are lightly browned. Set the baking sheet on a rack and cool for 3 minutes, until the cookies are firm enough to move. Transfer the cookies to a rack to cool.

8. Roll, cut, bake, and cool the second piece of dough in the same fashion. Store the cookies in a tightly covered tin or jar at room temperature for up to three days.

Sandwich Cookies:

Spread a layer of jam or melted chocolate over the bottoms of half of the cookies. Top each with another cookie (bottom-side down), and press lightly. Refrigerate until the filling is firm, 15 to 20 minutes.

Black and White Cookies:

Dip half of each cookie into melted chocolate. Refrigerate until the chocolate is set, 15 to 20 minutes. Or dip into chocolate first, then into finely chopped nuts or dried, shredded coconut.

Fancy Thins:

Dip the tines of a fork into melted chocolate and allow the chocolate to drip on the cookies, creating a freeform design.

I Fixed My Favorite
Peanut Butter Cookies

Yield: 30 (2-inch) cookies
See photo facing page 97.

¾ cup light natural cane sugar

½ cup unbleached white flour

¼ cup plus 1 tablespoon whole wheat pastry flour

½ teaspoon baking soda

¼ teaspoon baking powder

⅛ teaspoon salt

½ cup smooth peanut butter, at room temperature

3 tablespoons canola oil

¼ cup soymilk

2 teaspoons vanilla extract

1 teaspoon apple cider vinegar

While I did remember that traditional peanut butter cookie recipes contain eggs, I had forgotten how much (read lots!) butter or margarine was in them too. Nut butter contains enough fat on its own so that very little additional oil is needed in this recipe. And believe me, this much-lower-fat version is the real deal.

1. Position a rack in the middle of the oven and preheat to 350 degrees. Line two baking sheets with parchment paper.

2. Place a wire mesh strainer over a medium bowl. Add ½ cup of the sugar, the white flour, pastry flour, baking soda, baking powder, and salt to the strainer. Tap the strainer against the palm of your hand to sift the ingredients into the bowl. Stir with a wire whisk to distribute the ingredients.

3. Combine the peanut butter, canola oil, soymilk, vanilla, and vinegar in a food processor. Pulse until the mixture is smooth; it will be very thick. Add the dry mixture to the peanut butter mixture and pulse a few times, only until the dough begins to hold together.

4. Transfer the dough to a bowl and press and squeeze with your hands until the dough is smooth and shiny.

5. Put the remaining ¼ cup sugar on a plate. Shape the dough into 1-inch balls. Roll the balls in the sugar and place 2 inches apart on the prepared sheets. Use

the back of the tines of a dinner fork to press each cookie horizontally, then vertically, to flatten them into the traditional peanut butter cookie shape.

6. Bake the cookies, one sheet at a time, for 8 to 10 minutes, until the cookies are lightly browned. The cookies will be soft, but will firm as they cool.

7. Set the baking sheet on a rack and cool for 3 minutes until the cookies are firm enough to move. Transfer the cookies to a rack to cool. Store in a tightly covered tin at room temperature for two to three days.

Tip: The cookies sometimes puff up during baking, making the crisscross pattern disappear. (This seems to happen sometimes but not always.) If this is the case, remove the cookies from the oven after 8 minutes, and press the design into the cookies again. Bake another minute or two.

Peanut Butter and Jelly Cookies:

Use your little finger to make an indentation in the center of each cookie. Fill each indentation with ½ teaspoon all-fruit jam. Bake the cookies for 12 to 13 minutes.

Peanut Butter and Chocolate Cookies:

Those of us who loved peanut butter candy cups will appreciate this variation. Use your little finger to make an indentation in the center of each cookie. Fill each indentation with a few nondairy chocolate chips.

Anise Almond Biscotti

Yield: 2 small logs (18 slices each)
See photo facing page 97.

2 tablespoons plus 2 teaspoons anise seeds

1 cup whole raw almonds, toasted (see page 23) and cooled

1¼ cups whole wheat pastry flour

¼ teaspoon salt

½ cup canola oil

½ cup maple syrup

1 tablespoon vanilla extract

1 teaspoon almond extract

⅓ cup light natural cane sugar, for shaping

Not too hard, not too sweet, and good to dunk, these biscotti will keep for two weeks (although they're so delicious, you'd better make a double batch if you want them to last this long!). Biscotti means "twice baked" in Italian, but I learned in Italy that the term biscotti is often used to designate cookies in general.

1. Toast the anise seeds lightly in a small dry skillet over low heat, stirring constantly until fragrant. Cool. Grind in a spice grinder or other small grinder until fine.

2. Grind the almonds to a fine meal in a blender or food processor. Place a wire mesh strainer over a medium bowl. Add the pastry flour, salt, and ground anise to the strainer. Tap the strainer against the palm of your hand to sift the ingredients into the bowl. Stir the ground almonds into the dry mixture.

3. Whisk the oil, maple syrup, and vanilla and almond extracts together in a small bowl until well blended. Pour into the dry mixture and stir until a dough forms. A small piece of dough should hold together when squeezed. Allow the dough to rest in the bowl at room temperature for 10 minutes.

4. Turn the dough out onto a piece of parchment paper and cut the dough in half using a long, sharp knife. Spread ½ of the sugar on the counter and roll one piece of the dough in the sugar, shaping into a log 11 to 12 inches long. Repeat with the other piece of dough. Wrap each log in plastic wrap, and refrigerate for 1 to 8 hours.

5. Position a rack in the middle of the oven and preheat the oven to 350 degrees. Line a baking sheet with parchment paper.

6. Unwrap the logs and place on the prepared baking sheet, 3 to 4 inches apart. Bake for 25 to 30 minutes, until firm and lightly browned. Slide the logs, still on the parchment paper, off the sheet and onto a rack to cool. To ensure neat and even slicing later, wrap the logs in plastic wrap and refrigerate about 1 hour, until chilled. The parchment paper can remain on the baking sheet for use in the next step.

7. To make and bake the biscotti, preheat the oven to 300 degrees. Use a serrated knife to cut diagonal slices, ¼ inch thick. (This creates the typical biscotti shape. Cut straight down or saw into the logs gently; experiment to see what creates the neatest slices.) Place the biscotti cut-side down on the parchment-lined baking sheet, and bake for 6 minutes. Remove the sheet from the oven and flip the biscotti over with tongs or a spatula. Bake for 5 to 6 minutes longer, until dry.

8. Cool the biscotti on a rack. Store in a tightly covered tin for two weeks or longer.

Tips: There is no baking powder or baking soda in the recipe so the logs do not expand, but the biscotti have a very nice texture, firm but not hard.

• The logs can be shaped and wrapped, then frozen, either raw or baked, for one month.

• Make a double batch and divide the dough into four pieces. Bake two logs and freeze the other two, well wrapped, for up to one month. Thaw and bake.

Anise is an herb thought to aid digestion. In fact, Bella Nicholas, an exceptional baker and dear friend who really likes these biscotti, keeps a bowl of anise seeds on her dining table.

Honey-Free Better Baklava

Sweet Syrup

2½ cups brown rice
   syrup

1½ cups water

1 cinnamon stick

1 whole clove

1 lemon, sliced

Half an orange, sliced

Baklava

4 cups walnuts, toasted
   (see page 23) and
   cooled

2 tablespoons plus 1½
   teaspoons ground
   cinnamon

½ to ⅔ cup canola oil

1 (1-pound) box phyllo (filo),
   at room temperature
   (see page 85)

While the cloying sweetness associated with traditional baklava has been lightened in this recipe and the honey eliminated, the resulting flaky triangles retain their Greek roots. The instructions below may look time-consuming, but the components are quickly made and can be prepared ahead of time. You will need two large clean kitchen towels to assemble the baklava. Baklava is a great dish to make for a crowd; it stays fresh for two days stored at room temperature.

To make the syrup, combine the rice syrup, water, cinnamon stick, clove, and lemon and orange slices in a large saucepan, and bring to a boil over medium heat. Reduce the heat and simmer for 30 minutes. Strain the syrup and discard the spices and fruit. Sweet Syrup can be made ahead and refrigerated for up to two weeks in a covered jar. Reheat before using.

1. To prepare the baklava, position a rack in the middle of the oven and preheat to 375 degrees. Oil a 2- to 3-inch-deep 9 x 13-inch baking pan.

2. Chop the nuts in a food processor until fine but not ground. Mix the nuts and 2 tablespoons of the cinnamon in a medium bowl.

3. Mix ½ cup canola oil with the remaining 1½ teaspoons cinnamon in a small bowl.

4. Wet two large kitchen towels and wring them dry. Place one towel on the counter. Unwrap the phyllo and unroll it onto the towel. Use a sharp knife to cut the phyllo to the size of the baking dish. Immediately cover the phyllo with the other damp towel.

5. To start layering, gently pick up two pieces of phyllo. Lay them in the baking dish. Brush the top sheet with the cinnamon-oil mixture. Add another two sheets and brush the top with the cinnamon-oil mix. Continue layering, brushing every second sheet with the cinnamon-oil mix until 10 sheets of phyllo are in the pan. Spread half the nut mixture over the phyllo. Add 4 more sheets of phyllo, continuing to brush every other piece with the cinnamon-oil mix. Spread the remaining nut mixture on top, and layer 10 more sheets of phyllo, oiling every other sheet. Oil the top sheet of phyllo.

6. Use a long, sharp knife to cut the baklava into quarters, and cut each section into 4 squares. Cut each square in half diagonally to make 2 triangles. Make sure to cut all the way to the bottom.

7. Bake for 50 to 60 minutes until golden brown and puffed. Cool for 10 minutes. If the syrup has cooled or has been made ahead and refrigerated, bring it to a simmer in a medium saucepan. Pour over the baklava.

Working with Phyllo Dough

Phyllo dough is not as hard to work with as you may think. The ultra-thin dough does dry out quickly, but keeping it covered with damp (not wet) kitchen towels or with plastic wrap eliminates that problem. Fresh phyllo is fantastic and can be found in some Greek bakeries or ordered by mail (see Resources for Ingredients and Equipment, page 210), but frozen phyllo works very well. Both types must be brought to room temperature before you begin to make the baklava layers.

• Defrost a box of frozen phyllo in the refrigerator 8 to 12 hours. Remove the phyllo from the refrigerator 30 minutes to 1 hour before you are ready to assemble your recipe.

• Trim the edges of the phyllo with sharp scissors or a sharp, long knife before you begin to make layers. Brush the oil lightly between the layers; too much oil creates a greasy result.

Apricot Currant Nut and Oat Bars

Yield: one 8 x 8-inch pan (12 to 16 pieces)

2 cups unsweetened dried apricots (about 2/3 pound)

½ cup currants

1 (2-inch) strip orange zest

1 cup orange or apple juice

1 cup rolled oats

6 tablespoons pecans, toasted (see page 23) and cooled

½ cup whole wheat pastry flour

½ cup unbleached white flour

1 teaspoon ground cinnamon

¼ teaspoon baking powder

¼ teaspoon salt

4 to 5 tablespoons canola oil

5 tablespoons maple syrup

1 tablespoon brown rice syrup

1 teaspoon vanilla extract

½ teaspoon almond extract

3 tablespoons dark whole cane sugar

Dried apricots are pitted, unpeeled apricot halves that have had a large percentage of their moisture removed. They are a great source of vitamin A, iron, and calcium, but you will want to make these bars simply because they taste so good.

1. Position a rack in the middle of the oven and preheat to 375 degrees. Oil an 8 x 8-inch baking pan.

2. Combine the apricots, currants, zest, and juice in a medium saucepan. Simmer over low heat until the fruit has absorbed almost all the juice. Set aside to cool.

3. Process the oats and half the pecans in a food processor until coarsely ground. Transfer to a medium bowl.

4. Place a wire mesh strainer over a medium bowl. Add the pastry flour, white flour, cinnamon, baking powder, and salt into the strainer. Tap the strainer against the palm of your hand to sift the ingredients into the bowl. Stir the ingredients with a whisk to combine.

5. Mix 4 tablespoons of the oil, the maple syrup, rice syrup, and vanilla and almond extracts in a small bowl until well combined. Pour into the dry mixture and stir until the mixture holds together when squeezed. Add the remaining tablespoon oil if needed to make the dough moister.

6. Put half of the dough into the prepared pan. To prevent the dough from sticking to your fingers, place a piece of plastic wrap over it before pressing it evenly into the bottom of the pan. Bake for 15 minutes. Remove the pan from the oven and cool 10 minutes.

7. Remove the zest from the fruit and spoon the fruit over the crust. Crumble the remaining dough on top, and sprinkle with the remaining pecans and the dark whole cane sugar. Bake for 25 to 30 minutes, until the topping is golden brown. Place the pan on a rack and cool to room temperature or refrigerate before cutting in order to make the neatest cuts.

8. Cut into quarters and slice each quarter horizontally into three or four pieces. Use a narrow angled spatula to remove the bars from the pan. The first piece may break (it can be your sample piece) but the rest will remove easily.

Fruit Nut and Oat Bars:

Replace the apricots and currants with an equal quantity of other dried fruit.

Dried Apricots

Dried apricots are a healthful food but are routinely sprayed (as are other dried fruits) with sulfites, which can cause deadly reactions in asthmatics and others who suffer from sulfite allergies. Choose sulfite-free apricots whenever possible (check the label).

You can usually estimate there to be 8 to 12 apricots to a pound of dried fruit.

Carob Fudge Brownies

Yield: one 9 x 9-inch pan (8 to 16 pieces)

1¼ cups whole wheat pastry flour

¾ cup roasted or raw carob powder

½ cup unbleached white flour

¼ cup arrowroot

1½ teaspoons baking powder

1 teaspoon ground cinnamon

½ teaspoon salt

¼ teaspoon baking soda

⅓ cup canola oil

¾ cup maple syrup

2 teaspoons molasses or barley malt

⅓ cup soymilk

¼ cup prune purée (recipe follows) or apple butter

1 tablespoon vanilla extract

1 teaspoon almond extract

⅓ cup walnuts, toasted (see page 23), cooled, and chopped

⅓ cup currants

Carob Cashew Frosting (page 90)

Spread a layer of Carob Cashew Frosting on these rich-tasting brownies. Wrap and store them in the freezer—the brownies defrost quickly.

1. Position a rack in the middle of the oven and preheat to 350 degrees. Oil a 9 x 9-inch baking pan.

2. Place a wire mesh strainer over a medium bowl. Add the pastry flour, carob powder, white flour, arrowroot, baking powder, cinnamon, salt, and baking soda to the strainer. Tap the strainer against the palm of your hand to sift the ingredients into the bowl. Stir with a wire whisk to distribute the ingredients.

3. Whisk the oil, maple syrup, molasses or barley malt, soymilk, prune purée, and vanilla and almond extracts in a separate bowl until no lumps of prune purée remain and the mixture is well blended. Pour into the dry mixture and stir until smooth. Stir the walnuts and currants into the batter. Spread the batter into the prepared pan; it will be thick.

4. Bake for 20 to 25 minutes, until the top looks puffed and dry. A tester inserted into the center should have some moist crumbs on it. Don't overbake or the brownies will be dry.

5. Remove the pan from the oven and cool on a rack for 10 minutes. Keep in the pan and frost the brownies while they are warm with Carob Cashew Frosting.

Prune Purée

Yield: ⅔ to 1 cup

1 cup (6 ounces) pitted
   prunes, coarsely
   chopped

1 cup minus 1 table-
   spoon water

Additional water as
   needed

1. Put the prunes into a heat proof bowl. Bring the water to a boil and pour over the prunes. Set aside for 15 to 30 minutes until the prunes are soft.

2. Combine the prunes and soaking water in a blender. Blend at high speed until the puree is completely smooth, adding additional water, a tablespoon at a time, if needed. Use immediately, or place in an airtight container and store for up to three weeks in the refrigerator.

Carob Cashew Frosting

Yield: ¾ cup

5 tablespoons maple syrup

3 tablespoons brown rice syrup

½ teaspoon apple cider vinegar

¼ cup roasted or raw carob powder, sifted

Dash salt

⅓ cup smooth cashew butter

1 tablespoon vanilla extract

½ teaspoon almond extract

I was pleasantly surprised by the good taste and sheen of this frosting. You may be surprised to see vinegar listed as an ingredient; it adds a slight caramel note to the syrups.

1. Combine the maple syrup and rice syrup in a small saucepan with high sides. Bring to a boil over medium heat, stirring a few times. Reduce the heat to low. Add the vinegar and simmer 1 minute.

2. Whisk the carob slowly into the simmering syrup. Simmer 3 to 4 minutes, whisking frequently until the carob is dissolved.

3. Remove the saucepan from the heat, and add the salt, cashew butter, and vanilla and almond extracts, stirring until smooth. Pour the frosting into a shallow pan and cool to room temperature.

4. If the frosting is thick and creamy enough to spread easily, frost the brownies. If the frosting is too thin, refrigerate it for about 30 minutes, until thickened.

Tip: The frosting can be made up to two days ahead and refrigerated until needed. Stir vigorously with a wooden spoon before using.

Super Fudge Low Fat Brownies

See photo facing page 96.

Yield: one 9 x 9-inch pan (8 to 16 pieces)

¾ cup whole wheat pastry flour

½ cup unbleached white flour

2 tablespoons arrowroot

1 cup unsweetened Dutch-process cocoa

¼ cup dark whole cane sugar

¼ cup light natural cane sugar

1 teaspoon baking powder

½ teaspoon baking soda

½ teaspoon sea salt

3 tablespoons canola oil

1 cup maple syrup

⅓ cup prune purée (page 89)

2 tablespoons water

2 teaspoons vanilla extract

½ cup nondairy chocolate chips

⅓ cup walnuts, toasted, cooled and coarsely chopped, (see page 23) (optional)

Presenting the perfect brownie, fudgy, dense, a little gooey and deeply chocolate. I still can't believe these are low in fat. After one taste, a student said there was a new star in heaven with my name on it. I don't know about that, but I do know the prune purée, which replaces most of the fat (and adds a healthy dose of fiber), makes this miracle of a brownie possible.

1. Position a rack in the middle of the oven and preheat to 350 degrees. Oil a 9 x 9-inch pan.

2. Place a wire mesh strainer over a medium bowl. Add the pastry flour, white flour, arrowroot, cocoa, cane sugars, baking soda, baking powder, and salt to the strainer. Tap the strainer against the palm of your hand to sift the ingredients into the bowl. Stir with a wire whisk to distribute the ingredients.

3. Whisk the oil, maple syrup, prune purée, water and vanilla in a separate bowl until no lumps of prune purée remain and the mixture is well blended. The batter will be thick. Pour into the dry ingredients and stir until smooth. Stir the chips and walnuts, if using, into the batter.

4. Spread the batter into the prepared pan evenly. Bake for 17 to 18 minutes, until the top looks dry and set, and the sides of the brownies have pulled away from the sides slightly. A tester inserted into the center will be coated with very moist cake, but the cake will not feel gummy. Do not over bake or the brownies will be dry. The brownies will firm as they cool and when they are chilled.

5. Place the pan on a rack and cool to room temperature. Cover the pan with plastic wrap and refrigerate or freeze the brownies before cutting; cold brownies slice neatly.

No Bake Fruit and Nut Energy Bites (Wheat Free)

⅓ cup plus 1 table-spoon raisins

¼ cup unsweetened dried apricots

¼ cup pitted dates

½ cup pecans, toasted (see page 23), cooled, and finely chopped

¼ cup unsweetened shredded dried coconut, toasted (see page 23) and cooled

1 teaspoon minced orange zest (optional)

½ to 3 teaspoons orange juice, more if needed

Carry a few of these nutrient–dense treats with you for the times you need an energy boost.

1. Chop the raisins, apricots, and dates into small pieces on a dry cutting board, using a heavy knife.

2. Combine the fruit, pecans, coconut, and zest, if using, in a medium bowl. Add the juice ½ teaspoon at a time until the mixture holds together.

3. Shape into 1½-inch balls. Wrap individually in plastic wrap or store in a zipper-lock plastic bag or airtight container. Keep at room temperature for up to 3 days.

Tips: If the fruit is very sticky, flour your knife before chopping, or use kitchen shears or scissors.

• Any kind of fruit juice can be used, as very little is needed.

Chapter 4... Great Good Cobblers, Crisps, Biscuits, Muffins, and More

Introducing New Old-Fashioned Desserts

Great Good Cobblers, Crisps, Slumps, Grunts . . .

This category of recipes is composed of combinations of seasonal fruits and a variety of toppings, baked in the oven or cooked on the stove until the fruit is bubbling and the topping is golden and set. There are no bottom crusts to roll or press, and the recipes don't require the same precision needed for making cakes and pies. Substituting different fruit and topping combinations from those listed in the recipes is definitely encouraged.

Homey and old-fashioned, these are desserts dating from colonial times, likely devised to use an abundance of apples, leftover biscuits, and bits of bread. They are fantastic as a group, but traditional versions are made with unhealthful ingredients (solid shortening, including lard and butter, and heaps of white sugar) that had to go. The revised nondairy and egg-free Great Good Desserts versions feature nutritious ingredients, but the recipes stay true to their roots and, most importantly, taste fantastic.

Which is Which?

Interesting folklore surrounds the names of baked fruit dishes, which are often interchanged and interpreted differently depending on the recipe source. But the basic components remain constant: fruit filling and a quickly mixed topping.

- *Brown Betties:* Buttered bread crumbs (or diced bread) layered with applesauce.
- *Buckles:* Originally these were yellow cakes with blueberries baked into them and sprinkled with streusel-like crumbs. Keep a Blueberry Slump (page 100) in the pan for a few hours, and it will transform into a buckle.
- *Cobblers:* Fruit fillings baked in the oven under sugar-dusted, biscuit-style dough.
- *Crisps:* Fruit fillings baked in the oven and topped with a crunchy mix of flour, sugar, spice, fat, and usually rolled oats
- *Crumbles:* Essentially crisps minus the oats.
- *Slumps and Grunts:* Different names for the same thing, these are fruit fillings cooked in a tightly covered saucepan on the stove under a layer of soft biscuit batter. The biscuits actually steam as they slump (or grunt) into the filling.
- *Pandowdies:* Traditionally sliced apples baked under a piece of pie dough; the crust is cut into squares and pressed (or dowdyed) into the hot filling. You will find a recipe for a Pear Currant Pandowdy in the pie and tart chapter (page 175).

Biscuits, Muffins, and More Naturally

There can also be confusion about baking powder breads:

- *Biscuits and scones* are close relatives. Scones contain more sugar than biscuits and are shaped differently.

- *Muffins*, like cupcakes, are baked in special pans; some muffin batter can be baked in loaf pans, as well, to make quick breads. As noted in the section on essential equipment (see page 31), the recipes in this book use standard pans. Be aware that the jumbo muffins sold in many markets are often so huge that one muffin is at least two servings; they are calorie-loaded, cholesterol-laden, white sugar bombs. On the other hand, with no milk, no butter, no eggs, and no white sugar, our nondairy, egg-free, naturally sweetened versions are terrific, not heavy.

The Secrets to Making Perfect Nondairy, Egg-Free, New Old-Fashioned Desserts

- Think like a pastry chef and get prepared before you start. Read the recipe all the way through, and organize yourself for baking. Gather and prepare all the ingredients needed. Nuts, oats, seeds, and coconut, often used in these recipes, need to be toasted (page 23) and cooled.

- Use fresh, seasonal, flavorful fruit; organic is always the best choice. Visit local farm stands and farmers' markets if you are able to; it is fun and informative. Fruit must be washed, cut, or otherwise processed.

- To avoid dry or tough results, mix the batters for biscuit dough, scones, quick breads, and muffins lightly, only until the ingredients are moistened.

- Combine some apples, pears, and cranberries with a sweetener and spices in autumn.

- As the recipes indicate, summer fruits and berries make superb versions, but a small amount of starch is often added to lightly thicken the fruit juices.

- Fruit fillings can be made ahead, covered, and refrigerated 8 to 12 hours. Allow the filling to return to room temperature while the oven is preheating.

- Position the racks in the correct section of the oven for the recipe.

- Preheat the oven and use an oven thermometer to check the accuracy of the temperature.

- Prepare the baking pans according to the recipe.

- Use the appropriate measuring cups: nested, straight-sided cups for dry ingredients and glass or plastic cups with pouring spouts for liquid ones.

- Use a wire mesh strainer to sift the dry ingredients into a bowl.

Blueberry Peach Cobbler

Yield: 8 to 10 servings

Filling

⅓ to ½ cup light natural cane sugar, depending on the sweetness of the fruit

¼ cup dark whole cane sugar

1 tablespoon arrowroot

Dash salt

2 cups fresh blueberries, picked over, rinsed, and patted dry

4 ripe peaches (4 cups thick slices, see tip)

Finely grated zest of half an orange (optional)

Blueberries and peaches are a gorgeous and scrumptious combination. Select dark, firm blueberries and fragrant, juicy peaches.

1. Position a rack in the middle of the oven and preheat to 400 degrees. Line a baking sheet with parchment paper. Oil a 9-inch deep-dish pie pan or a 2-quart ovenproof baking dish. Place the baking dish on the prepared baking sheet for easier handling and to catch any juice that may bubble over.

2. To make the filling, combine the sugar, dark whole cane sugar, arrowroot, and salt in a large bowl, and stir to mix. Add the berries, peaches, and zest, if using, and toss gently until well coated. Spoon the fruit into the prepared baking dish, and cover with a piece of parchment paper cut to fit. Cover with aluminum foil and bake for 20 to 25 minutes, until the fruit is bubbling. Make the topping when the filling has baked for 20 minutes.

Super Fudge Low Fat Brownies, p. 91

Topping

¼ cup dark whole cane sugar

½ cup whole wheat pastry flour

½ cup unbleached white flour

¼ cup light natural cane sugar

1½ teaspoons baking powder

¼ teaspoon salt

¼ teaspoon ground cinnamon

⅛ teaspoon baking soda

¼ cup canola oil

¼ cup soymilk or rice milk

¼ cup orange juice

1 teaspoon vanilla extract

¼ teaspoon apple cider vinegar

I Fixed My Favorite Peanut
   Butter Cookies, p. 80,
Vanilla Wafer Cookies, p. 78,
Orange Ginger Crisps, p. 72,
Anise Almond Biscotti, p. 82

3. To make the topping, blend the dark whole cane sugar in a blender for a minute or two until fine. Place a wire mesh strainer over a medium bowl. Add the pastry flour, white flour, sugar, dark whole cane sugar, baking powder, salt, cinnamon, and baking soda to the strainer. Tap the strainer against the palm of your hand to sift the ingredients into the bowl. Stir with a wire whisk to distribute the ingredients.

4. In a separate medium bowl, whisk the oil, soymilk, orange juice, vanilla, and vinegar until well blended. Pour into the dry mixture and stir only until the batter is blended. Spoon the batter evenly over the hot fruit. Return the baking dish to the oven and bake for 15 to 18 minutes, until lightly browned and set.

Tip: Because peach skins tend to be thick, the fruit is often peeled before cooking. I have found an easy way to eliminate the time-consuming process of blanching and cooling the fruit, which is the standard way the skins are removed. Instead of peeling the peaches, use a fork to prick the skin lightly all over (do this over a bowl to catch any juice); slice and use.

Apricot Blackberry Raspberry Crisp

Yield: 6 to 8 servings

Topping

¾ cup whole wheat pastry flour

½ cup dark whole cane sugar

½ teaspoon ground cinnamon

¼ teaspoon baking powder

¼ teaspoon salt

¼ teaspoon ground nutmeg

½ cup rolled oats, toasted (see page 23) and cooled

¼ cup maple syrup

3 to 4 tablespoons canola oil

2 teaspoons vanilla extract

The colors of the fruit in the baked crisp are gorgeous and the flavors a delightful medley.

1. To make the topping, place a wire mesh strainer over a medium bowl. Add the pastry flour, dark whole cane sugar, cinnamon, baking powder, salt, and nutmeg to the strainer. Tap the strainer against the palm of your hand to sift the ingredients into the bowl. Add the oats directly to the bowl and stir to distribute the ingredients.

2. In a small bowl, combine the maple syrup, 3 tablespoons of the oil, and the vanilla, and stir until well blended. Pour over the oat mixture and stir until coated. The topping should be damp, but not soaking wet. Add the remaining tablespoon of oil, if needed to add more moisture.

Filling

1 pound fresh apricots, halved and pitted (about 3 cups)

2 cups fresh blackberries, picked over and rinsed

2 cups fresh raspberries, picked over and rinsed

4 to 6 tablespoons light natural cane sugar, depending on the sweetness of the fruit

Dash salt

Tip: The topping can be made ahead and stored in zipper-lock bags. Freeze for up to one month. Defrost slightly at room temperature and proceed with the recipe.

3. To make the filling, combine the fruit, 3 tablespoons of the sugar, and the salt in a large bowl, and stir until the fruit is coated. Add sugar to the fruit mixture to taste. Set the fruit aside for 15 minutes, mixing it gently once or twice. (The sugar will pull some delicious concentrated juice out of the fruit.) Taste the fruit mixture and add more sugar if desired.

4. Position a rack in the middle of the oven and preheat to 350 degrees. Line a baking sheet with parchment paper and place a 9-inch deep-dish pie pan or 2-quart baking dish on the sheet.

5. Spoon the fruit and accumulated juice into the baking dish. Sprinkle the crisp topping over the fruit and bake for 35 to 40 minutes, until the topping is browned and firm to the touch. If the topping appears to be browning too quickly, cover the baking dish with parchment paper, then aluminum foil.

Blueberry Slump

Filling

3 cups fresh blueberries, picked over and rinsed

1/3 cup light natural cane sugar

1/2 cup orange juice

1/2 cup water

This recipe appeared in my first book, Great Good Desserts Naturally, *and is so popular I had to include it again. The liquid in the filling steams the biscuits, which slump or grunt into the filling. In any case, made with a mere 1 1/2 tablespoons of oil, this very low-fat version of blueberry slump is excellent. Reduce the sugar to 1/4 cup if the berries are very sweet.*

To make the filling, combine the berries, sugar, juice, and water in a 9-inch saucepan with a tight-fitting lid; the pan should be at least 3 inches deep. Bring to a boil over medium heat, stirring a few times. Reduce the heat to low and simmer for 2 to 3 minutes. Cover the saucepan and keep the fruit warm over the lowest heat while you make the batter. Just before the batter is ready, bring the fruit to a simmer.

Pear Cranberry Slump:

Substitute equal amounts of cranberries and diced ripe pears for the blueberries. Replace the water with 1/2 cup maple syrup.

Biscuit Batter

¼ cup plus 3 tablespoons light natural cane sugar

2½ teaspoons ground cinnamon

½ cup plain or vanilla soymilk

1 teaspoon lemon juice or apple cider vinegar

½ cup whole wheat pastry flour

½ cup unbleached white flour

2 teaspoons baking powder

1 teaspoon baking soda

¼ teaspoon salt

1½ tablespoons canola oil

¾ teaspoon vanilla extract

Finely grated zest of half an orange

1. Mix 3 tablespoons of the sugar and 2 teaspoons of the cinnamon in a small bowl. Set aside.

2. To make the biscuit batter, mix the soymilk and lemon juice in a small bowl, and set aside for 2 to 3 minutes. (This is called clabbering and will result in a buttermilk substitute.) Bring the fruit back to a simmer.

3. Place a wire mesh strainer over a medium bowl. Add the pastry flour, white flour, remaining ¼ cup sugar, baking powder, baking soda, remaining ½ teaspoon cinnamon, and salt to the strainer. Tap the strainer against the palm of your hand to sift the ingredients into the bowl. Stir with a wire whisk to distribute the ingredients.

4. Stir the oil, vanilla, and zest into the clabbered soymilk. Pour into the dry mixture, and stir with a wooden spoon just until a soft batter forms.

5. Use two tablespoons to drop rounds of batter on the simmering fruit. Cover the saucepan with a tight-fitting lid or piece of aluminum foil, bring back to a simmer, and cook over low heat, without uncovering, for 25 minutes. The biscuits will feel firm to the touch when they are cooked.

6. Cool for 10 minutes and sprinkle with the reserved cinnamon sugar. Serve warm with a few spoonfuls of Silken Cashew Cream (page 60), if you like.

7. Store leftover slump covered with waxed paper or parchment paper, and keep at room temperature for up to 24 hours. After a few hours, the biscuit will have absorbed most of the liquid in the berry sauce, making the slump more like a buckle; different but still delicious.

Apple Walnut Cobbler

(Wheat Free)

Yield: 6 to 8 servings

Filling

5 tablespoons maple syrup

1 tablespoon arrowroot

2 teaspoons fresh lemon juice

Dash salt

5 cups apple slices, unpeeled or peeled (about 2 pounds)

Maple syrup brushed on the warm cobbler adds color and shine to the otherwise pale topping. And don't save this excellent cobbler for wheat-sensitive people only; everyone will like it.

1. Position a rack in the middle of the oven and preheat to 350 degrees. Lightly oil a 9-inch deep-dish pie pan or 2-quart baking dish.

2. To make the filling, mix the maple syrup and arrowroot in a large bowl until well blended. Add the lemon juice and salt. Add the apples and toss until coated. Spoon the apples into the prepared baking dish.

Topping

½ cup oat flour (see page 75)

2 tablespoons dark whole cane sugar

¾ teaspoon ground cinnamon

¾ teaspoon baking powder

¼ teaspoon baking soda

Dash salt

3 tablespoons canola oil

3 tablespoons maple syrup

6 tablespoons soymilk or rice milk

1 teaspoon vanilla extract

3. To make the topping, combine the oat flour, dark whole cane sugar, cinnamon, baking powder, baking soda, and salt in a medium bowl, and stir to mix.

4. Combine the oil with 1 tablespoon of the maple syrup in a small bowl. Add the soymilk and vanilla, and mix until well blended. Pour into the oat mixture and mix until a soft dough forms.

5. Spoon the topping over the fruit and bake for 25 to 35 minutes, until the topping is firm and the fruit is bubbling. Remove from the oven and brush with the remaining 2 tablespoons maple syrup. Cool about 5 minutes and serve warm from the baking dish.

Apple Brown Betty Babies

Yield: 8 servings

4 cups unsweetened applesauce, homemade or commercially prepared

⅓ cup apple juice or cider

2 to 4 tablespoons dark whole cane sugar

½ teaspoon ground cinnamon

3 to 4 tablespoons maple syrup

2 cups fine, dry cake crumbs

Tips: Betties can be baked ahead and reheated in a 325- degree oven before serving.

• The amounts of applesauce and crumbs are approximate. Use more or less as you wish. You can also use finely ground cookie crumbs or whole grain bread crumbs instead of cake crumbs.

The Pilgrims brought apples to the New World in 1620, and brown Betty was probably created to use up an abundant crop. Although Betties are traditionally layered with buttered bread crumbs or cubed bread, our Betty is more flavorful because it is made using cake crumbs. Dark Moist Spice Cake (page 136) is an excellent choice, but any other cake will do.

1. Position a rack in the middle of the oven and preheat to 350 degrees. Lightly oil 8 small (1-cup) ramekins or custard cups, and place them on a baking sheet.

2. Combine the applesauce, juice, 2 tablespoons of the dark whole cane sugar, and the cinnamon in a small bowl, and stir until mixed. Add more dark whole cane sugar to the applesauce mixture to taste.

3. Combine 3 tablespoons of the maple syrup and the cake crumbs in a small bowl, and stir until the crumbs are very damp but not soaking wet. Add the remaining tablespoon of maple syrup, if needed to moisten.

4. Scatter 1½ to 2 tablespoons of crumb mixture on the bottom of each ramekin. Spoon ½ cup applesauce mixture over the crumbs, and sprinkle with another 1½ to 2 tablespoons crumbs. Bake until the applesauce is bubbling, about 20 minutes.

5. Cool a few minutes. Serve warm with a tablespoon of any tofu whip or nut cream.

Fresh Raspberry Betty

Yield: 6 servings

3 pints fresh raspberries, picked over and rinsed (see page 65)

4 tablespoons light natural cane sugar, or more to taste

1 cup coarse whole wheat bread crumbs

2 tablespoons dark whole cane sugar

2 tablespoons maple syrup

1 tablespoon canola oil

½ teaspoon vanilla extract

Here is a different Betty to enjoy during the short but sweet raspberry season.

1. Position a rack in the middle of the oven and preheat to 375 degrees.

2. Toss the berries with the sugar in a 9-inch deep-dish pie pan or other baking dish, and set aside while you make the topping.

3. Combine the bread crumbs and dark whole cane sugar in a small bowl. Combine the maple syrup, oil, and vanilla in a separate small bowl, and stir until well blended. Pour the syrup mixture over the crumb mixture and toss until the crumbs are well coated.

4. Scatter the crumbs over the berries and bake 20 to 30 minutes, until the berries are bubbling. Cool about 10 minutes before serving.

Tips: If the crumb topping is browning too fast, cover with a piece of parchment paper.

• If you are using frozen berries, bake this 10 minutes longer.

Good Cornbread

Yield: one 9 x 9-inch pan (8 to 12 pieces)

1 cup fresh yellow
cornmeal

½ cup whole wheat
pastry flour

½ cup unbleached
white flour

1 tablespoon plus 1½
teaspoons baking
powder

¼ teaspoon salt

½ cup plus 2 table-
spoons soymilk

½ cup water

3 tablespoons
maple syrup

2 tablespoons
canola oil

2 teaspoons
vanilla extract

Make cornbread from scratch—it's fast and you'll avoid the refined, enriched cornmeal, sugar, and additives found in boxed mixes.

1. Position a rack in the middle of the oven and preheat to 425 degrees. Oil a 9 x 9-inch baking pan.

2. Place a wire mesh strainer over a medium bowl. Add the cornmeal, pastry flour, white flour, baking powder, and salt to the strainer. Tap the strainer against the palm of your hand to sift the ingredients into the bowl. Stir with a wire whisk to distribute the ingredients.

3. Whisk the soymilk, water, maple syrup, canola oil, and vanilla in a small bowl until well blended. Pour into the dry mixture and whisk only until the batter is smooth. The batter will drop off a spoon like heavy pancake batter. Pour into the prepared pan and smooth the top.

4. Bake for 15 to 18 minutes, until golden brown and a tester inserted into the center comes out clean or with a few moist crumbs.

5. Cool the pan on a rack for 10 minutes before cutting. Tightly wrap the cornbread with plastic wrap and store at room temperature for up to one day.

Tips: Serve the cornbread with maple syrup or jam, if desired.

• Brush the cornbread with maple syrup while it is cooling if you like a sweeter taste and moister cornbread.

• It is important to buy fresh, whole cornmeal and to store the cornmeal in the refrigerator or freezer to prevent the oils in it from becoming rancid.

Blueberry Cornbread:

Mix 1 cup blueberries into the batter

Savory Cornbread:

Mix 1 cup corn kernels, sautéed bell pepper, or onions into the batter.

Skillet Cornbread:

Oil a cast-iron pan. Preheat the pan in the oven before adding the batter, and bake as directed. The sides and bottom of the cornbread will be dark and crusty.

Corn Muffins:

Position a rack in the upper third of the oven and preheat to 400 degrees. Oil 10 cups in a standard muffin tin or cornstick pan, fill them three-quarters full, and bake for 15 to 20 minutes. Pour $\frac{1}{3}$ cup water into any empty cups to ensure even baking.

Banana Currant Walnut Cornmeal Pancakes

Yield: 15 to 16 pancakes

1 cup fresh yellow cornmeal

½ cup whole wheat pastry flour

½ cup unbleached white flour

1 tablespoon plus 1½ teaspoons baking powder

¼ teaspoon salt

1 cup soymilk

¼ cup water

3 tablespoons maple syrup

2 tablespoons canola oil

2 teaspoons vanilla extract

1 to 2 ripe bananas, sliced

½ cup currants

½ cup walnuts

Maple syrup or Maple Cider Syrup (page 62), warm, for serving

I find ordinary pancakes heavy and boring. The taste of these pancakes is brightened by the nutty taste of cornmeal.

1. Place a wire mesh strainer over a medium bowl. Add the cornmeal, pastry flour, white flour, baking powder, and salt to the strainer. Tap the strainer against the palm of your hand to sift the ingredients into the bowl. Pour any cornmeal left in the strainer into the bowl. Stir with a whisk to distribute the ingredients.

2. Whisk the soymilk, water, maple syrup, oil, and vanilla in a separate medium bowl until well blended. Pour into the dry mixture and stir only until the batter is smooth.

3. Oil a griddle or heavy skillet, and heat until drops of water sprinkled on the griddle bounce around. Pour about ¼ cup of the batter on the griddle to make each pancake, leaving 2 inches between pancakes. Let the batter set a few seconds, then arrange a few banana slices, currants, and walnuts on each. When bubbles start to form on the top of the pancakes and the edges just begin to dry, flip the pancakes over and cook the other side about a minute, until lightly browned. Serve with warm maple syrup or Maple Cider Syrup.

Tip: Just for fun, arrange the fruit to resemble a face, with banana eyes, a walnut nose, and currants in the shape of a smile.

Blueberry Cornmeal Pancakes:
Stir 1 cup blueberries into the batter.

Baking Powder Biscuits

Yield: 9 to 10 (2-inch) biscuits

1½ cups unbleached white flour, plus more for kneading

½ cup whole wheat pastry flour

2 tablespoons light natural cane sugar

4 teaspoons baking powder

⅛ teaspoon salt

⅓ cup ice-cold canola oil (place a jar in the freezer for 45 minutes)

¼ cup ice-cold soymilk

My mother–in–law, Wini Costigan, was an exceptional baker, my mentor and inspiration. I wanted to make her biscuits, but of course, without the Crisco she used. I am happy with these and hope you are too. This is the biscuit to use for Strawberry Shortcakes (page 112).

1. Position a rack in the middle of the oven and preheat to 425 degrees. Line a baking sheet with parchment paper.

2. Place a wire mesh strainer over a medium bowl. Add the white flour, pastry flour, sugar, baking powder, and salt to the strainer. Tap the strainer against the palm of your hand to sift the ingredients into the bowl. Stir with a rubber spatula to distribute the ingredients. Make a well in the center of the mixture.

3. Whisk the oil and soymilk until well blended in a small bowl, and pour into the center of the dry mixture. Stir only until combined (any longer and the biscuits will be tough). The dough will be soft. Keep the dough in the bowl.

4. Knead the dough in the bowl; it will be very sticky and soft. Flour your hands and sprinkle the dough with 1 tablespoon flour. Lift the dough, turn it over, and sprinkle with another tablespoon of flour. Work the flour into the dough, continuing to turn the dough and adding very small amounts of flour until the dough is no longer sticky; it will still be quite soft.

Lightly dust the counter with flour. Turn the dough out on the flour and pat into a round about 10 inches wide and ½ inch thick.

5. Press a 2-inch biscuit cutter straight down into the dough, making the cuts as close together as possible. Place the biscuits on the prepared sheet 1 inch apart.

6. Bake for 9 to 10 minutes, until the biscuits have risen and are lightly browned. Remove from the oven and wrap the biscuits loosely in kitchen towels. Cool for 10 minutes before serving. The biscuits taste best the day they are made, but can be kept at room temperature 8 to 12 hours in an airtight plastic container or zipper-lock plastic bag. Freeze the biscuits, tightly wrapped, for up to two weeks.

Tips: Pat and press the scraps from cutting biscuits into a round, and cut one more batch.

• Brush the top of the biscuits with maple syrup after they have cooled for 5 minutes to add color and sweetness.

Strawberry Shortcakes

Yield: 6 shortcakes
See photo facing page 144.

3 cups fresh strawberries, picked over, rinsed, and patted dry

⅓ cup light natural cane sugar, or more to taste

2 cups Strawberry Tofu Cream (page 59)

6 Baking Powder Biscuits (page 110)

Perhaps the quintessential summertime dessert, strawberry shortcakes are composed of split biscuits that are covered with juicy, sweetened sliced strawberries and topped with whipped cream. This Great Good version features nondairy Baking Powder Biscuits and Strawberry Tofu Cream. All the components can be made in advance.

1. Hull the strawberries and cut them into thick slices. Combine the berries with the sugar in a medium bowl, and toss to coat. Push down on some of the berries until slightly crushed. Set aside at room temperature for 20 to 30 minutes, stirring twice.

2. Mix 1 cup of the sugared berries into the Strawberry Tofu Cream.

3. To assemble the shortcakes, slice the biscuits in half and place the bottom half of each biscuit on a serving plate. Spoon some of the sugared berries (and accumulated juice) over the biscuit bottom, and cover with the top piece and some Strawberry Tofu Cream.

Chocolate Strawberry Shortcakes:

Pour some Ultimate Chocolate Sauce (page 63) over the bottom halves of the biscuits. Spoon some of the sugared berries over the chocolate sauce. Cover with the top halves and some of the Strawberry Tofu Cream. Drizzle more chocolate sauce over the tops.

Any-Fruit Shortcakes:

Strawberry shortcake is traditional, but many other fruit and cream combinations are excellent too. Replace the strawberries with an equal quantity of a combination of other berries or fruit. Sliced peaches and blackberries pair well with Soft Orange Tofu Cream (page 58), for example.

How to Choose, Wash, and Store Fresh Strawberries

Strawberries are best used within two to three days of picking. Pick out any bruised or spoiled berries, cover loosely with a piece of waxed paper or paper towel, and store them unwashed in the refrigerator. Do not crowd or press the berries. Wash them as close to recipe preparation (or eating) as possible, and hull them after washing. A pint box of medium-sized berries yields 2 cups.

The nutritional profile of strawberries is first-rate, and they are low in calories. Because strawberries can be heavily contaminated with pesticides (the Environmental Working Group detected as many as 36 different pesticides on 90 percent of the strawberries they tested), do seek out and buy local seasonal organic berries.

Currant Scones

2 tablespoons dark
  whole cane sugar

1 cup whole wheat
  pastry flour

1 cup unbleached white
  flour, plus more for
  kneading

½ cup light natural
  cane sugar

4 teaspoons baking
  powder

¾ teaspoon ground
  cinnamon

¼ teaspoon salt

⅓ cup plus 1 tablespoon
  ice-cold canola oil
  (place a jar in the
  freezer for 45
  minutes)

¼ cup ice-cold soymilk

1 teaspoon vanilla
  extract

1 cup currants

Scones are made like biscuits, but more sugar is added and they are baked at a lower temperature. Typically, the dough is cut into triangles. The yield depends entirely on the size of scone you choose to make.

1. Blend the dark whole cane sugar in a blender for a minute or two until fine. Place a wire mesh strainer over a medium bowl. Add the pastry flour, white flour, sugar, dark whole cane sugar, baking powder, cinnamon, and salt to the strainer. Tap the strainer against the palm of your hand to sift the ingredients into the bowl. Stir with a wire whisk to distribute the ingredients, and make a well in the center.

2. Whisk the oil, soymilk, and vanilla in a small bowl until well blended, and pour into the center of the dry mixture. Stir with a rubber spatula only until combined (any longer and the scones will be tough). Gently stir the currants into the dough. Dust the dough with flour and turn out of the bowl onto a flour-dusted counter or board.

3. Divide the dough in half with a dough scraper or sharp knife, and work with one piece at a time. Flour your hands and knead by lifting the farthest edge of the dough toward the center. Press it into the center, turn the dough a quarter turn, and repeat until the dough is no longer sticky, using only as much flour as necessary. Pat each piece into a square about ½ inch thick, wrap in plastic wrap, and refrigerate for 30 minutes to allow the gluten to relax.

4. While the dough is resting, position a rack in the middle of the oven and preheat to 400 degrees. Line a baking sheet with parchment paper.

5. Remove one piece of dough from the refrigerator, unwrap, and cut into four triangles. Repeat with the second piece. Place the scones 2 inches apart on the prepared sheet. Brush the tops lightly with maple syrup. Bake for 9 to 10 minutes.

Chocolate Chip Scones:

Replace the currants with an equal quantity of nondairy chocolate chips. These are very, very good when split and spread with peanut butter.

Apricot Apple Carrot Muffins

Yield: 12 to 13 standard muffins

⅓ cup unsweetened dried apricots, cut into small pieces

½ cup apricot juice or apple juice

1 cup whole wheat pastry flour

1 cup unbleached white flour

2 tablespoons dark whole cane sugar

2 teaspoons baking powder

2 teaspoons baking soda

2 teaspoons ground cinnamon

½ teaspoon salt

½ teaspoon ground nutmeg

½ teaspoon ground cloves

The combination of apricot and apple makes moist muffins, packed with nutritious ingredients.

1. Position a rack in the upper third of the oven and preheat to 400 degrees. Oil the top and cups of a 12-cup standard muffin tin.

2. Soak the apricots in the juice for 15 minutes, or until they are plump. Drain the apricots in a small strainer set over a measuring cup and reserve 6 tablespoons of the juice.

3. Place a wire mesh strainer over a medium bowl. Add the pastry flour, white flour, dark whole cane sugar, baking powder, baking soda, cinnamon, salt, nutmeg, and cloves to the strainer. Tap the strainer against the palm of your hand to sift the ingredients into the bowl. Stir with a wire whisk to distribute the ingredients.

1 cup maple syrup

½ cup unsweetened applesauce, homemade or commercially prepared

⅓ cup soymilk

3 tablespoons canola oil

1 tablespoon apple cider vinegar

1 teaspoon vanilla extract

1 cup peeled, shredded carrots (2 to 3 carrots), firmly packed

4. Whisk the maple syrup, applesauce, soymilk, oil, vinegar, vanilla, and the reserved apricot juice in a separate medium bowl until well blended. Pour into the dry mixture, and stir only until the batter is smooth. Gently stir in the carrots and drained apricots.

5. Allow the batter to thicken for 1 minute (it will look like it is growing). Spoon the batter into the prepared tin, filling each cup about three-quarters full. (Any leftover batter can be baked in an oiled custard cup.) Bake for 12 to 13 minutes, until well risen (the tops will be domed), golden brown, and a tester inserted into the middle of a muffin comes out clean.

6. Cool the tin on a rack for 10 minutes. Carefully run a thin knife between the muffins and the inside of the cups, and lift each muffin onto the rack to cool completely.

Spiced Pumpkin Cranberry Muffins

Yield: 12 to 13 standard muffins

1 cup whole wheat pastry flour

1 cup unbleached white flour

1½ teaspoons baking powder

1 teaspoon baking soda

¼ teaspoon salt

¾ teaspoon ground cinnamon

¼ teaspoon ground ginger

¼ teaspoon ground nutmeg

⅔ cup soymilk

2 teaspoons fresh lemon juice or apple cider vinegar

Pumpkin and cranberries are a perfect pairing. Try these moist, maple syrup–sweetened muffins with a cup of warm apple cider.

1. Position a rack in the upper third of the oven and pre-heat to 400 degrees. Oil the top and cups of a 12-cup standard muffin tin. (The cups can be lined with paper liners but the top of the tin must still be oiled.)

2. To make the muffins, place a wire mesh strainer over a medium bowl. Add the pastry flour, white flour, baking powder, baking soda, salt, cinnamon, ginger, and nutmeg to the strainer. Tap the strainer against the palm of your hand to sift the ingredients into the bowl. Stir with a wire whisk to distribute the ingredients.

3. Mix the soymilk and lemon juice in a small bowl and set aside for 2 to 3 minutes. (This is called clabbering and will result in a buttermilk substitute.)

1 cup plus 1 tablespoon Spiced Pumpkin Purée (page 55), cooled

¼ cup canola oil

¼ cup maple syrup

2 teaspoons vanilla extract

¼ teaspoon orange extract

2 teaspoons apple cider vinegar

½ cup dried cranberries

4. Combine the pumpkin purée, oil, maple syrup, vanilla and orange extracts, and vinegar in a medium bowl. Add the clabbered soymilk and whisk until well blended. Pour into the dry mixture and stir only until the batter is smooth. Stir the cranberries into the batter and spoon into the prepared tin, filling each cup three-quarters full. (Any leftover batter can be baked in an oiled custard cup.)

5. Bake for 12 to 13 minutes, or until the muffins are well risen (the tops will be domed), golden brown, and a tester inserted into the middle of a muffin comes out clean.

6. Cool the tin on a rack for 10 minutes. Carefully run a thin knife between the muffins and the inside of the cups, and lift each muffin onto the rack to cool completely.

Pumpkin Pecan Bread

Yield: one 8½ x 4½-inch loaf (8 or more slices)

1 cup whole wheat pastry flour

1 cup unbleached white flour

1½ teaspoons baking powder

1 teaspoon baking soda

¼ teaspoon salt

¾ teaspoon ground cinnamon

¼ teaspoon ground ginger

¼ teaspoon ground nutmeg

⅔ cup soymilk

2 teaspoons fresh lemon juice or apple cider vinegar

1. Position a rack in the middle of the oven and preheat to 375 degrees. Oil an 8½ x 4½-inch loaf pan.

2. Place a wire mesh strainer over a medium bowl. Add the pastry flour, white flour, baking powder, baking soda, salt, cinnamon, ginger, and nutmeg to the strainer. Tap the strainer against the palm of your hand to sift the ingredients into the bowl. Stir with a wire whisk to distribute the ingredients.

3. Mix the soymilk and lemon juice in a small bowl and set aside for 2 to 3 minutes. (This is called clabbering and will result in a buttermilk substitute.)

1 cup plus 1 tablespoon
  Spiced Pumpkin Purée
  (page 55), cooled

¼ cup canola oil

¼ cup maple syrup

2 teaspoons vanilla
  extract

¼ teaspoon orange
  extract

2 teaspoons apple cider
  vinegar

½ cup pecans, toasted
  (see page 23), cooled,
  and coarsely chopped

4. Combine the pumpkin purée, oil, maple syrup, vanilla and orange extracts, and vinegar in a medium bowl. Add the clabbered soymilk and whisk until well blended. Pour into the dry mixture and stir only until the batter is smooth. Stir the pecans into the batter, spoon into the prepared loaf pan, and bake for 33 to 35 minutes, until the loaf is well risen and the sides of the loaf have started to pull away from the pan. Brush the loaf with maple syrup and bake 6 minutes longer.

5. Cool completely. Wrap in plastic wrap and let rest 4 hours before slicing. (For an even more flavorful loaf, let rest 8 to 12 hours before slicing.)

Banana Walnut Bread

Yield: one 8½ x 4½-inch loaf (8 or more slices)

¾ cup whole wheat pastry flour

¼ cup unbleached white flour

1 teaspoon baking powder

1 teaspoon ground cinnamon

½ teaspoon baking soda

¼ teaspoon salt

2 ripe bananas, well mashed (about ⅔ cup)

½ cup plus 1 tablespoon soymilk

½ cup maple syrup, plus more for brushing on the loaf

3 tablespoons canola oil

1 teaspoon vanilla extract

1 teaspoon apple cider vinegar

½ cup walnuts, toasted (see page 23), cooled, and coarsely chopped

Buy extra bananas and when they are very ripe, but not over-ripe, make some good banana bread. Try a slice toasted and spread with jam.

1. Position a rack in the middle of the oven and preheat to 375 degrees. Oil an 8½ x 4½-inch loaf pan.

2. Place a wire mesh strainer over a medium bowl. Add the pastry flour, white flour, baking powder, cinnamon, baking soda, and salt to the strainer. Tap the strainer against the palm of your hand to sift the ingredients into the bowl. Stir with a wire whisk to distribute the ingredients.

3. Combine the bananas, soymilk, maple syrup, oil, vanilla, and vinegar in a separate medium bowl, and mix until well blended. Pour into the dry mixture and stir only until the batter is smooth. Stir the walnuts into the batter and spoon into the prepared pan. Smooth the top and bake for 35 minutes, until set and golden brown.

4. Remove the pan from the oven, and reduce the heat to 350 degrees. Bush the top of the loaf with maple syrup. Return the loaf to the oven and bake 10 minutes longer, until a cake tester inserted in the center of the loaf (check a few spots) is almost clean and does not feel gummy. Bake longer, if needed.

5. Cool the pan on a rack for 10 minutes. Run a thin knife between the loaf and the pan, and turn the loaf out onto the rack. Cool completely and wrap tightly in plastic wrap. Store the loaf at room temperature for about 8 hours before slicing.

Tip: In order to make a flavorful banana bread, the bananas must be ripe. However when bananas are overripe, soft, or bruised, they have a slightly fermented odor and taste, so use them at their peak.

Banana Walnut Muffins

Yield: 6 standard muffins

1. Position a rack in the upper third of the oven and preheat to 400 degrees. Oil 6 cups and the top of a standard muffin tin.

2. Make the Banana Walnut Bread recipe. Fill the prepared muffin cups two-thirds full. Pour ⅓ cup water into any empty cups to ensure even baking.

3. Bake for 12 to 13 minutes. Cool the tin on a rack for 10 minutes. Carefully run a thin knife between the muffins and the inside of the cups, and lift each onto the rack to cool completely. Keep the muffins in a covered container for up to two days. Freeze for up to one month.

Hearty Oat and Jam Muffins

Yield: 12 standard muffins

1¼ cups whole wheat pastry flour

2 tablespoons dark whole cane sugar or maple sugar

2½ teaspoons baking powder

1½ teaspoons ground cinnamon

½ teaspoon baking soda

¼ teaspoon salt

6 tablespoons rolled oats, toasted (see page 23) and cooled

¼ cup raisins or currants

¼ cup sesame seeds, toasted (see page 23) and cooled

Feel good, not guilty, when you grab one of these moist, hearty, maple syrup–sweetened muffins, chock–full of healthful whole foods ingredients. These are good breakfast or anytime muffins with a nice surprise of all–fruit jam. Not only do they taste delicious, they provide plenty of energy with very little fat. Be sure to use very ripe bananas for the best flavor.

1. Position a rack in the upper third of the oven and preheat to 375 degrees. Oil the cups and tops of a standard 12-cup muffin tin. Insert paper liners into the cups if you like, but the top of the tin must be oiled.

2. Place a wire mesh strainer over a medium bowl. Add the pastry flour, dark whole cane sugar, baking powder, cinnamon, baking soda, and salt to the strainer. Tap the strainer against the palm of your hand to sift the ingredients into the bowl. Stir the oats, raisins and sesame seeds into the dry mixture. Make a well in the center.

1 cup soymilk

2 ripe bananas, well mashed (about ⅔ cup)

6 tablespoons maple syrup

2 tablespoons canola oil

4 teaspoons apple cider vinegar

2 teaspoons vanilla extract

2 tablespoons all-fruit jam

3. Combine the soymilk, mashed bananas, maple syrup, oil, vinegar, and vanilla in a separate medium bowl and stir until well blended.

4. Pour into the dry mixture and stir with a rubber spatula only until the ingredients are moistened. Allow the batter to rest about 30 seconds. Spoon the batter into the prepared muffin tin, filling each cup three-quarters full. Quickly drop about ½ teaspoon jam in the center of each muffin.

5. Bake for 15 to 16 minutes, or until the muffins are golden brown and firm and a tester inserted into the middle of a muffin comes out clean or with a few crumbs. (The tops of these muffins are flat, not domed.)

6. Cool the tin on a rack for 10 minutes. Carefully run a thin knife between the muffins and the inside of the cups. Lift each muffin onto the rack to cool completely. Store the muffins in a tightly covered plastic container or zipper-lock plastic bag for a day or two, or freeze them for up to a month.

Chapter 5... Great Good Cakes, Fillings, Frostings, and Glazes

Introducing Great Good Cakes Naturally

Some of the cakes in this chapter are baked and served plain, straight from the pan, but most are layers that are filled and frosted with a cream, icing, or glaze. You don't have to make everything at one time, though, because virtually all the cakes can be made ahead and frozen, and the fillings, frostings, and glazes can be made from one day to several days before the cake is served. In fact, the fillings and frostings need time to chill and set, and the cakes must be chilled before they are assembled.

Yes! We can have our birthday cakes and eat them too!

Instead of the bleached flours, saturated fats, dairy, eggs, and other refined ingredients found in traditional recipes, the recipes in this chapter use unrefined flours, canola oil, pure maple syrup, pure vanilla extract, and aluminum-free baking powder. The cakes are light and tender, and look every bit like their traditional counterparts.

Be creative and have fun. Improvise with unexpected results. Did the cake break? Make a trifle or serve pieces covered with cream and fruit. Does the cake taste good except for the center, which didn't quite bake through? Cut out the center and call it a Bundt cake. Feel free to mix and match the cakes, fillings, and frostings in this chapter to make them your own.

The Secrets to Baking Perfect Nondairy, Egg-Free Cakes

Follow the rules for making perfect cakes every time.

• Think like a pastry chef and get prepared before you start. Read the recipe all the way through and make sure you understand the directions. Organize yourself for baking. Gather and prepare all the ingredients needed. Use fresh, good quality ingredients.

• Position the racks in the correct section of the oven for the recipe. Cakes bake best on the middle rack of the oven but can be rotated if the upper rack needs to be used.

• Preheat the oven and use an oven thermometer to check the accuracy of the temperature.

• Prepare the baking pans according to the recipe. Oil the pans with canola oil and line the bottoms with parchment paper cut to fit.

• Use the appropriate measuring cups: nested, straight-sided cups for dry ingredients and glass or plastic cups with pouring spouts for liquid ones.

• Use a wire mesh strainer to sift the dry ingredients into a bowl.

• Never, ever combine the dry and liquid ingredients until you are ready to put the cake into the oven.

• Test the cake after the minimum baking time has elapsed, not before. A finished (fully baked) cake has risen, the center looks dry, and the sides will have started to pull away from the pan. A cake tester inserted in the center will come out dry or with a few moist, but not wet, crumbs.

• Unless the recipe says otherwise, cool the cake in the pan set on a rack for 10 minutes, then run a thin knife between the cake and the inside of the pan. Invert the cake on another rack and allow it to cool completely. Hot cakes are fragile and easily broken. For best results, chill the layers in the refrigerator for 1 to 8 hours. Cold cakes are easier to fill and frost.

Virtuous Vanilla Cake

Yield: one 8-inch two-layer cake (8 to 10 servings)

1 cup whole wheat pastry flour

1 cup unbleached white flour

1 teaspoon baking powder

1 teaspoon baking soda

½ teaspoon salt

½ teaspoon ground cinnamon

¼ cup plus 1 tablespoon canola oil

¾ cup plus 2 tablespoons maple syrup

¾ cup vanilla rice milk or soymilk

3 tablespoons vanilla extract

2 teaspoons apple cider vinegar

2 cups Cashew Cream Icing (page 132), or any other frosting of your choice

This is dairy–free baking at its simplest. Learn to make this delicious, not too sweet, easily varied recipe, and you'll have mastered the method for baking perfect maple syrup–sweetened cakes. I have followed the recipe with one for Vanilla Cinnamon Frosting, but any frosting, filling, pudding, or glaze can be used with this cake (which is also delicious served plain).

1. Position a rack in the middle of the oven and preheat to 350 degrees. Oil two 8-inch round cake pans. Line the bottoms with parchment paper cut to fit.

2. Place a wire mesh strainer over a medium bowl. Add the pastry flour, white flour, baking powder, baking soda, salt, and cinnamon to the strainer. Tap the strainer against the palm of your hand to sift the ingredients into the bowl. Stir with a wire whisk to distribute the ingredients.

3. Whisk the oil, maple syrup, rice milk, vanilla, and vinegar in a separate medium bowl until well blended. Pour into the dry mixture and stir with a whisk until the batter is smooth.

4. Divide the batter evenly between the two pans, and smooth the tops with a spatula. Tap the pans lightly on the counter to eliminate air bubbles.

5. Bake for 20 to 25 minutes, until the tops of the cakes are golden, the sides have started to pull away from the pans, and a cake tester inserted in the centers comes out clean or with only a few moist crumbs.

6. Cool the pans on racks for 10 minutes. Run a thin knife between the cake and the inside of the pan. Invert each layer onto a rack. Remove the pans and carefully peel off the parchment paper. Invert the layers again top-side up onto a rack. Cool completely.

7. To protect the layers from cracking or break-ing, slide a cardboard circle under each one. Wrap the layers in plastic wrap, and refriger-ate 1 to 8 hours, until cold, before filling and frosting.

8. To assemble the cake, place one of the layers on a flat plate. Spread ½ cup of the frosting over the top. Place the other layer bottom side up onto the top of the cake and remove the cardboard. Spread with ⅔ cup of the frosting. Ice the sides of the cake with the remaining frosting.

Tip: To freeze the cake layers, wrap them tightly in plastic wrap and overwrap with aluminum foil. Freeze for up to one month. Unwrap and defrost at room temperature.

Nut, Fruit, or Chocolate Chip Vanilla Cake:

Stir ½ cup coarsely chopped toasted nuts, dried fruit, toasted coconut, or chocolate chips into the batter.

Virtuous Vanilla Bundt Cake:

Pour the batter into a well-oiled 6-cup Bundt pan. Increase the baking time to 35 to 40 minutes.

Cashew Cream Icing

Yield: 2⅓ cups

1 (14- to 16-ounce) package firm tofu (2 cups), blanched and drained (see page 29)

1 tablespoon plus 1 teaspoon canola oil

2 teaspoons freshly squeezed lemon juice

½ cup light natural cane sugar or maple sugar

¼ cup dark whole cane sugar, finely ground (see page 18)

¼ teaspoon ground cinnamon

⅛ teaspoon salt

1 tablespoon vanilla extract

½ cup smooth cashew butter

This simple icing is spread between the layers and on the top of the cake, but not on the sides. The cream needs to chill in the refrigerator for it to thicken before it is used, so plan ahead.

1. Crumble the tofu into a blender or food processor, and process with the oil and lemon juice for 5 minutes until puréed, stopping a few times to clean the sides of the jar or bowl. Add the sugars, cinnamon, salt, and vanilla and process about 5 minutes longer, until perfectly smooth and creamy. (Machines with stronger motors will cream the mixture more quickly.) Add the cashew butter and pulse the machine on and off four or five times, then process until incorporated.

2. Spoon the cream icing into a shallow container, cover, and refrigerate for 1 hour. If the icing is thick enough to spread, fill the cake and frost the top. If not, chill longer, up to 24 hours.

Chocolate Ganache

Yield: 2⅔ to 3 cups

1 pound nondairy semisweet or bittersweet chocolate, very finely chopped

1½ cups soy creamer

Classic ganache is made with heavy cream and chocolate. The proportions of cream and chocolate differ based on the use; a pouring ganache for a glaze is thinner than one made for a frosting or a truffle. Soy creamer makes a good substitute for the cream, but make sure you use a good-quality chocolate with a flavor you like, because it's the taste of the chocolate that comes through. If you cannot find soy creamer, use good-tasting full-fat soymilk and add 1 teaspoon of vanilla extract.

1. Place the chocolate in a medium heatproof bowl.

2. Pour the creamer into a small saucepan and bring to a boil over medium heat. Pour over the chocolate and let sit for 1 minute. Stir gently with a rubber spatula until the chocolate melts and is smooth.

3. Pour the ganache into a shallow dish and refrigerate for 1 to 2 hours, or until firm enough to spread. The ganache will keep for one week in the refrigerator. Warm to spreading consistency in a heatproof bowl over simmering water, stirring until it can be spread.

Vanilla Cupcakes

Yield: 10 cupcakes

1 cup plus 2 tablespoons whole wheat pastry flour

¾ cup plus 2 table-spoons unbleached white flour

¼ cup dark whole cane sugar or light natural cane sugar

1 teaspoon baking powder

1 teaspoon baking soda

½ teaspoon salt

½ teaspoon ground cinnamon

⅓ cup canola oil

¾ cup plus 2 tablespoons maple syrup

¾ cup vanilla rice milk or soymilk

2 tablespoons vanilla extract

2 teaspoons apple cider vinegar

We all need a good cupcake recipe for school birthdays, bake sales, and snacks. This vanilla cupcake fits the bill. Serve plain or ice with Chocolate Ganache (page 133) or the cream or glaze of your choice.

1. Position a rack in the upper third of the oven and preheat to 375 degrees. Oil the cups and top of a standard muffin tin.

2. Place a wire mesh strainer over a medium bowl. Add the pastry flour, white flour, dark whole cane sugar, baking powder, baking soda, salt, and cinnamon to the strainer. Tap the strainer against the palm of your hand to sift the ingredients into the bowl. Stir with a wire whisk to distribute the ingredients.

3. Whisk the oil, maple syrup, rice milk, vanilla, and vinegar in a separate bowl until well blended. Pour into the dry mixture and stir with a whisk until the batter is smooth.

4. Divide the batter among the prepared cups, filling each about three-quarters full. Pour ⅓ cup water into any empty cups to ensure even baking.

5. Bake for 13 to 15 minutes, until the cupcakes are well risen (the tops will be domed), golden, and a cake tester inserted into the middle comes out clean or with only a few moist crumbs.

6. Cool the tin on a rack for 10 minutes. Carefully run a thin knife between the cupcakes and the inside of the cups, and lift onto a rack. Cool completely before icing. Keep the finished cupcakes refrigerated for up to two days, but serve at room temperature.

Tips: The cupcakes can be baked in paper liners (the sides of the cupcakes will be softer), but be sure to oil the top of the tin.

• Unfrosted cupcakes can be kept at room temperature in a covered container for one day or frozen in an airtight container (wrap the container in aluminum foil) for up to a month. Defrost and ice while still cold, but serve at room temperature.

• To vary the presentation, ice with Island Coconut Cream Filling and Frosting (page 144).

Coconut Cupcakes:

Replace the rice milk with an equal quantity of coconut milk.

Dark Moist Spice Cake

Yield: one 8 x 8-inch pan (8 servings)

½ cup whole wheat pastry flour

½ cup unbleached white flour

1 teaspoon baking powder

½ teaspoon baking soda

2½ teaspoons ground ginger

½ teaspoon ground cinnamon

¼ teaspoon salt

⅛ teaspoon ground cloves

Dash dry mustard

Your kitchen will fill with a divine spicy scent, reminiscent of gingerbread, when you bake this cake. This flavorful cake is good served plain, but Ginger Tofu Whip (page 57) is a perfect complement.

1. Position a rack in the middle of the oven and preheat to 350 degrees. Oil an 8 x 8-inch pan. Line the bottom with parchment paper cut to fit.

2. Place a wire mesh strainer over a medium bowl. Add the pastry flour, white flour, baking powder, baking soda, ginger, cinnamon, salt, cloves, and dry mustard to the strainer. Tap the strainer against the palm of your hand to sift the ingredients into the bowl. Stir with a wire whisk to distribute the ingredients.

½ cup plus 1 tablespoon soymilk

2½ tablespoons canola oil

6 tablespoons maple syrup

¼ cup molasses (not blackstrap)

1 tablespoon vanilla extract

1¼ teaspoons apple cider vinegar

Tip: The amount of batter in the pan is scant, but the cake rises considerably. If you'd like to make a layer cake, double the recipe and bake in two 9-inch round cake pans that are at least 2 inches deep.

3. Whisk the soymilk, oil, maple syrup, molasses, vanilla, and vinegar in a separate medium bowl until well blended. Pour into the dry mixture and stir with a whisk until the batter is smooth.

4. Pour the batter into the prepared pan and smooth the top with a spatula. Bake for 20 to 25 minutes, until the cake is well risen and its sides are starting to pull away from the pan, and a cake tester inserted in the center comes out clean or with only a few moist crumbs.

5. Cool the pan on a rack for 10 minutes. Run a thin knife between the cake and the inside of the pan. Invert onto a rack. Remove the pan and carefully peel off the parchment paper. Invert the layer again top-side up on a rack. Cool completely.

Lovely Light Lemon Cake

Yield: one 8-inch two-layer cake (8 to 10 servings)

1 cup whole wheat pastry flour

1 cup unbleached white flour

1½ teaspoons baking powder

1 teaspoon baking soda

½ teaspoon salt

⅓ cup canola oil

¾ cup maple syrup

⅔ cup rice milk or soymilk

¼ cup plus 2 tablespoons fresh lemon juice

1 teaspoon minced lemon zest

1½ teaspoons vanilla extract

½ teaspoon lemon extract

2 teaspoons apple cider vinegar

Luscious Lemony Cream (page 140)

Lemony, moist, and tender, this maple syrup–sweetened cake is filled and iced with a smooth sweet–tart cream.

1. Position a rack in the middle of the oven and preheat to 350 degrees. Oil two 8-inch round cake pans and line the bottoms with parchment paper cut to fit.

2. Place a wire mesh strainer over a medium bowl. Add the pastry flour, white flour, baking powder, baking soda, and salt to the strainer. Tap the strainer against the palm of your hand to sift the ingredients into the bowl. Stir with a wire whisk to distribute the ingredients.

3. Whisk the oil, maple syrup, rice milk, lemon juice and zest, vanilla and lemon extracts, and vinegar in a separate medium bowl until well blended. Pour into the dry mixture and stir with a whisk until the batter is smooth. The batter will be fairly thick.

4. Divide the batter evenly between the two prepared pans and smooth the tops with a spatula. Tap the pans lightly on the counter to eliminate air bubbles.

5. Bake for 20 to 25 minutes, or until the tops of the cakes are golden, the sides have started to pull away from the pans, and a cake tester inserted in the centers comes out clean or with only a few moist crumbs.

6. Cool the pans on racks for 10 minutes. Run a thin knife between each cake and the inside of the pan. Invert each layer on a rack. Remove the pans and carefully peel off the parchment paper. Invert the layers again topside up on a rack. Cool completely.

7. To protect the layers from cracking or breaking, slide a cardboard circle (or another flat surface) under each one. Wrap the layers in plastic wrap, and refrigerate 1 to 8 hours, until cold, before filling and frosting.

8. To assemble the cake, place one of the layers on a flat plate. Spread $\frac{1}{2}$ cup of the frosting over the top. Remove the other layer from the cardboard onto the top of the cake and press lightly. Spread with $\frac{2}{3}$ cup of the frosting. Ice the sides of the cake with the remaining frosting.

Lemon Poppy Seed Cake:

Add $\frac{1}{3}$ cup toasted poppy seeds to the batter.

Chocolate Glazed Lemon Torte:

Chocolate and lemon make a wonderful combination of flavors. Choose Chocolate Ganache (page 133) or Ultimate Chocolate Icing (page 147) for this cake. In season, add a border of fresh raspberries for a truly spectacular special-occasion cake.

Lemon Cake with Glazed Cranberries:

For a stunning fall or winter holiday cake, spoon Maple Glazed Cranberries (page 141) over either a frosted or unfrosted lemon cake.

Luscious Lemony Cream

Yield: about 2 cups

2 dashes turmeric

¼ cup plus 1 table-spoon fresh lemon juice

1 (14- to 16-ounce) package firm tofu (2 cups), blanched (page 29) and drained

1 tablespoon canola oil

1 tablespoon smooth cashew butter

½ cup light natural cane sugar or maple sugar

½ teaspoon salt

Zest of 1 lemon, finely grated (about 2 tablespoons)

1½ teaspoons vanilla extract

½ teaspoon lemon extract

Use only fresh lemon juice to make this sweet–tart cream. Bottled lemon juice has a medicinal taste and the result will be disappointing. The pinch of turmeric adds a nice "eggy" color.

1. Dissolve the turmeric in 1 tablespoon of the lemon juice.

2. Crumble the tofu into a blender or food processor. Add the oil and cashew butter, and process for 2 or 3 minutes, stopping several times to scrape down the sides of the jar or bowl. Add the sugar, salt, and remaining ¼ cup lemon juice, and process for 1 or 2 minutes until the mixture is smooth and creamy. Add the lemon zest, vanilla and lemon extracts, and the dissolved turmeric. Pulse the blender or processor a few times to mix.

3. Refrigerate the cream in a covered container for 4 to 8 hours to allow the flavors to blend. The cream will thicken slightly.

Maple Glazed Cranberries

Yield: 1 cup

1/3 cup maple syrup

1 cup fresh or frozen cranberries, picked over and rinsed

1/2 teaspoon orange extract

In spring and summer, replace the cranberries with fresh raspberries, if you like.

1. Bring the maple syrup to a boil in an 8-inch skillet with a heavy bottom. Stir the cranberries into the syrup and cook until the berries just begin to pop. Remove from the heat and add the orange extract.

2. Refrigerate the cranberries in a covered container for 1 hour or up to 2 days. Drain the cranberries before using; save the delicious syrup for drizzling over the serving plates.

Coconut Cloud Layer Cake

Yield: one 9-inch two-layer cake (10 to 15 servings)

2 cups unbleached white flour

2 teaspoons baking powder

2 teaspoons baking soda

½ teaspoon salt

⅓ cup canola oil

¾ cup plus 2 tablespoons maple syrup

¾ cup plus 2 tablespoons unsweetened coconut milk, stirred

1 tablespoon vanilla extract

1 teaspoon coconut extract

1 tablespoon apple cider vinegar

1 cup unsweetened shredded dried coconut, toasted (see page 23) and cooled

Island Coconut Cream Filling and Frosting (page 146)

My son Michael and his bride Linda were married on the island of Nevis. Shortly before I was to leave home for the wedding, I was surprised with a seemingly impossible task. Lovey, the Nevis baker famous for her coconut cake, had been asked to make individual layer cakes for the wedding, but the couple now wanted me to make a tiered creation. Happily, Lovey was open to collaboration. She filled and frosted layer upon layer of her cakes with soft coconut cream, while I managed to assemble the requisite tiers from Styrofoam rounds and canned icing I had packed at the last minute. We placed one of her round layer cakes on top of the assembled tiers, and added the bride and groom figures. When the bride and groom sliced the top layer and fed each other the traditional first piece, Lovey and I giggled at our secret—only the top layer of the beautiful cake was edible. The yummy cakes she'd made were cut in the kitchen and served from there. Her coconut cake is so outstanding that I was determined to create a nondairy and egg-free version when I returned home.

1. Position a rack in the middle of the oven and preheat to 350 degrees. Oil two 9-inch round cake pans and line the bottoms with parchment paper cut to fit.

2. Place a wire mesh strainer over a medium bowl. Add the flour, baking powder, baking soda, and salt to the strainer. Tap the strainer against the palm of your hand to sift the ingredients into the bowl. Stir with a wire whisk to distribute the ingredients.

3. Whisk the oil, maple syrup, coconut milk, vanilla and coconut extracts, and vinegar in a separate medium bowl until well blended. Pour into the dry mixture and stir with a whisk until the batter is smooth. Stir ½ cup of the coconut into the batter.

4. Divide the batter evenly between the two prepared pans, and smooth the tops with a spatula. Tap the pans lightly on the counter to eliminate air bubbles.

5. Bake for 20 to 30 minutes, or until the cakes have risen completely and the tops look dry, the sides have started to pull away from the pans, and a cake tester inserted in the centers of the cakes comes out clean or with only a few moist crumbs. (The tops will not brown.)

6. Cool the pans on racks for 10 minutes. Run a thin knife between the cakes and the pans and invert each layer on a rack. Remove the pans and carefully peel off the parchment paper. Invert again top-side up on a rack to cool completely.

7. To protect the layers from cracking or breaking, slide a cardboard circle (or another flat surface) under each one. Wrap the layers in plastic wrap, and refrigerate 1 to 8 hours, until cold, before filling and frosting.

8. To assemble the cake, place the layer on a cake decorating turntable or lazy Susan (or improvise to make an elevated surface).

recipe continues next page

Coconut Cloud Layer Cake

(continued)

9. Tuck strips of parchment paper or waxed paper under the outside edge of the cake to catch any frosting that may drop off, and spread the layer with about ⅔ cup of the frosting. Remove the second layer from the cardboard onto the top of the cake and spread with another ⅔ to 1 cup of the frosting. Spread the remaining frosting on the sides.

10. Chill the cake in the refrigerator for at least 2 hours then bring to room temperature before serving. Sprinkle the top of the cake with the remaining ½ cup toasted coconut, slice, and serve.

Strawberry Shortcakes, p. 112

Island Coconut Cream Filling and Frosting

Yield: about 3⅓ cups

3 tablespoons agar flakes

1 cup plus 3 tablespoons unsweetened coconut milk, stirred

2 tablespoons arrowroot

1½ (14- to 16-ounce) packages firm tofu (3 cups), blanched (see page 29) and drained

3 tablespoons canola oil

2 tablespoons fresh lime juice

¼ teaspoon salt

2 cups plus 2 tablespoons light natural cane sugar

1½ cups unsweetened shredded dried coconut

1 tablespoon vanilla extract

1½ teaspoons coconut extract

Big Orange Bundt Cake, p. 160

This recipe makes a splendid cream, soft yet firm enough to spread. It can also double as a delicious coconut cream pudding. Note that the shredded coconut in the filling is not toasted.

1. Put the agar in a small saucepan. Pour in 1 cup of the coconut milk but do not stir or heat. Set aside for 15 minutes or longer.

2. Combine the arrowroot and the remaining 3 tablespoons coconut milk in a small bowl. Stir with a fork to dissolve. Set aside.

3. Purée the tofu in a blender or food processor until smooth. Add the oil, lime juice, and salt, and process for 2 minutes, stopping several times to clean the sides of the jar or bowl with a spatula. Add the sugar in two batches and process for 3 to 4 minutes, again stopping the machine a few times to clean the sides. Add the coconut in two batches to the tofu mixture, then the vanilla and coconut extracts. Process until thoroughly mixed and creamy. Keep the tofu mixture in the bowl.

recipe continues next page

Cakes, Frostings, Glazes

Island Coconut Cream Filling and Frosting (continued)

4. To cook the agar, cover the saucepan with a lid and bring to a boil over medium heat. Uncover and remove from the heat. Stir vigorously. Cover and set aside for 3 to 4 minutes. Uncover and return the saucepan to the stove. Simmer over low heat, stirring vigorously with a heatproof spatula for 3 or 4 minutes. Most of the agar will be dissolved, but expect to see a few specks.

5. Stir the dissolved arrowroot with a fork again. Add to the simmering agar mixture, whisking continuously. This mixture will thicken instantly. Switch to a rubber spatula, and push down on the mixture to combine. The mixture will sputter rather than actually boil. As soon as you see some big bubbles breaking the surface remove the saucepan from the heat. (If you cook or stir arrowroot-thickened mixtures after they have boiled, they are likely to become thin again.) Spoon over the tofu cream and pulse the blender or processor a few times to mix.

6. Spoon the cream into a bowl. Cover and refrigerate 4 to 8 hours until the cream thickens. Stir gently before using.

Ultimate Chocolate Icing

Yield: about 2¼ cups (enough to fill and frost an 8- or 9-inch two-layer cake)

3 cups Ultimate Chocolate Sauce (page 63), freshly made or at room temperature

½ cup arrowroot

6 tablespoons cool water

2 teaspoons vanilla extract

Tips: Fill the used pan with hot water immediately. It will clean up easily.

• The icing can be made a day in advance, and refrigerated in a covered container. Stir it well before using.

Dark, shiny, and rich tasting (but low fat, thanks to the cocoa powder), this icing is suitable for people with nut and soy allergies. Chocolate burns easily and care must be taken to cook this icing until it thickens without burning the bottom. The trick to making this icing is to use a wide, shallow pan (an 8– to 9–inch sauté pan is perfect). This icing is similar to a glaze in texture.

1. Pour the chocolate sauce into a wide saucepan and bring to a simmer over low heat, stirring frequently with a rubber spatula. Be sure to stir the bottom and sides.

2. Combine the arrowroot with the water in a small bowl, and stir with a fork until thoroughly dissolved. Add to the simmering sauce, whisking constantly. The sauce may become lumpy, but will smooth as it is stirred. Cook over medium heat only until the sauce boils. (If you cook or stir arrowroot-thickened mixtures after they have boiled, they are likely to become thin again.) You will need to have patience cooking the sauce slowly to a boil. Remove the saucepan from the heat, add the vanilla, and continue to stir gently until the bubbling stops and the icing is smooth.

3. Spoon the icing into a shallow dish and cool to room temperature. Cover and refrigerate 1 hour, until cold and slightly thickened.

The Chocolate Cake
to Live For

Yield: one 9-inch two-layer cake (10 to 15 servings)

1 cup whole wheat pastry flour

1 cup unbleached white flour

½ cup plus 2 tablespoons unsweetened Dutch-process cocoa

½ cup light natural cane sugar

2 teaspoons baking powder

2 teaspoons baking soda

1 teaspoon salt

½ teaspoon ground cinnamon

½ cup canola oil

1 cup maple syrup

2 cups chocolate or vanilla soymilk

1 tablespoon vanilla extract

1 teaspoon almond extract

2 teaspoons apple cider vinegar

Ultimate Chocolate Icing (page 147)

This is an excellent, moist, rich tasting, deeply chocolate cake, guaranteed to satisfy even the most ardent chocoholic. It's easy and versatile too. Dense and fudgy, it always elicits the comment, "No way there's no dairy in this cake!" The cake with a fan club just had to be included again in this new edition.

1. Position a rack in the middle of the oven and preheat to 350 degrees. Oil the sides and bottom of two 9-inch round cake pans and line the bottoms with parchment paper cut to fit.

2. Place a wire mesh strainer over a medium bowl. Add the pastry flour, white flour, cocoa, sugar, baking powder, baking soda, salt, and cinnamon to the strainer. Tap the strainer against the palm of your hand to sift the ingredients into the bowl. Stir with a wire whisk to distribute the ingredients.

3. Whisk the oil, maple syrup, soymilk, vanilla and almond extracts, and vinegar in a separate medium bowl until well blended. Pour into the dry mixture and stir with a whisk until the batter is smooth. This batter is meant to be fairly thin.

4. Divide the batter evenly between the two prepared pans. Tap the pans lightly on the counter to eliminate air bubbles.

5. Bake for 25 to 30 minutes, or until the tops of the cakes are set, the sides have started to pull away from the pans, and a cake tester inserted in the centers of the cakes comes out clean or with only a few moist crumbs.

6. Cool the pans on wire racks for 10 minutes. Run a thin knife between the cake and the inside of the pan, and invert each layer onto a rack. Remove the pans and carefully peel off the parchment paper. Invert again topside up on a rack to cool completely.

7. To protect the layers from cracking or breaking, slide a cardboard circle (or another flat surface) under each one. Wrap the layers in plastic wrap, and refrigerate 1 to 8 hours, until cold, before filling and frosting.

8. While a decorating turntable (see Essential Equipment, page 31) is nice to have, it's not essential for this cake. To assemble the cake, place one of the layers bottom-side up on a serving plate. Tuck strips of parchment or waxed paper under the outside edge of the cake to catch any frosting that drips. Stir the icing and spread about ²⁄₃ cup on the layer. Set the second layer over it, topside up, and press down lightly. Use a wide knife or an offset spatula to ice the sides of the cake. Don't worry if it is not perfectly smooth at this point. Spread about 1 cup of the icing on the top of the cake, covering one section at a time. Push any extra icing off the top and onto the sides. Smooth the sides and top with the flat side of the knife or spatula.

9. Refrigerate the cake at least 1 hour before slicing. Remove the paper before serving.

Tips: This cake, unlike cakes frosted with tofu creams, can be iced, sliced, and frozen for up to two weeks. Place the slices in a flat, freezer-proof container cut-side down (they can be stacked in layers separated by a piece of parchment paper). Wrap the container in aluminum foil. Remove the cake slices from the container and defrost on plates at room temperature.

• Reducing the soymilk in the recipe from 2 cups to 1½ cups makes layers that are just slightly higher.

Colossal Chocolate Cake

Yield: one 9-inch 3-layer cake (12 to 18 servings)

Pictured on front cover

1½ cups whole wheat pastry flour

1½ cups unbleached white flour

1 tablespoon baking powder

1 tablespoon baking soda

1¼ teaspoons salt

¾ teaspoon ground cinnamon

¾ cup plus 3 tablespoons unsweetened Dutch-process cocoa

¾ cup light natural cane sugar

¾ cup canola oil

1½ cups maple syrup

2¼ cups chocolate or vanilla soymilk

4½ teaspoons vanilla extract

1½ teaspoons almond extract

1 tablespoon apple cider vinegar

This four–inch–high "wow" of a layer cake is not difficult to make, but the layers and cream need to be made several hours in advance, so plan accordingly.

1. Position a rack in the middle of the oven and another rack above it. Preheat to 350 degrees. Oil three 9-inch round cake pans, and line the bottoms with parchment paper cut to fit.

2. Follow the method for making, baking, and cooling The Chocolate Cake to Live For, page 148. Divide the batter evenly among the three prepared pans. Place two pans on the lower rack and center the remaining pan on the upper rack. Bake for 25 to 35 minutes.

3. To assemble the cake, cover a cake-decorating turntable or other elevated surface with a piece of parchment paper to catch any frosting that drops off the cake. Set the first layer on the turntable. Use a long serrated knife to level the tops of the layers, if needed. (Save any leftover pieces for snacking or making crumbs.)

Chocolate Cream Filling and Frosting (page 152)

Tips: If you do not have three 9-inch round cake pans, make two layers, following the recipe for The Chocolate Cake to Live For (page 148). Divide the recipe in half to make the third layer, or bake another full recipe and freeze the extra layer for another time.

• The cake can be covered with plastic wrap and refrigerated for 24 hours, or frozen for up to two weeks. If desired, you can freeze the cake in large, wrapped pieces; defrost unwrapped at room temperature.

4. Use an icing spatula to spread about 1½ cups of the frosting on the layer, covering a section at a time. (If the layer is uneven, spread more cream on the thinner areas.) Place another layer bottom-side up on the cream-covered layer, remove the cardboard, and spread with another 1½ cups of the cream.

5. Remove the third layer from the cardboard onto the top of the cake. Press down lightly and push one or two thin, long wooden skewers through the middle of the cake to keep the layers from slipping. Spread about 1½ cups frosting over the top, swirling as you go by pushing the spatula in and out of the cream. Push excess frosting off the top onto the sides, then frost the sides. After the sides are covered, you can spread additional frosting on the top.

6. The cake is ready to serve immediately but can be refrigerated for up to 24 hours. Use a long, sharp knife to slice the cake. Remove the skewers before slicing.

Chocolate Cream Filling and Frosting

Yield: 5½ to 6 cups (enough to fill and frost one 9-inch three-layer cake)

2 (14- to 16-ounce) packages silken tofu, or 3 (12.3-ounce) boxes extra-firm silken tofu (4 cups)

4 tablespoons canola oil

1 teaspoon salt

¾ cup light natural cane sugar

¾ cup unsweetened Dutch-process cocoa

4 teaspoons vanilla extract

18 ounces nondairy semisweet or bitter-sweet chocolate, melted (see page 21)

6 to 12 tablespoons chocolate, vanilla, or plain soymilk, if needed

Unless you have a food processor with at least an 8-cup bowl, make the cream in two or even three batches. Depending on the type of tofu you use, either the tofu will have to drain for 24 hours or the cream will have to chill for at least 6 hours, so this is a recipe to make ahead.

1. If you are using 14- to 16-ounce packages of silken tofu, set a wire mesh strainer over a bowl. Put the tofu in the strainer, cover with plastic wrap, and refrigerate for 24 hours. It is important to choose a bowl that allows the strainer to sit above the liquid that will accumulate. (Save the liquid to use in smoothies if you like. Draining the excess liquid helps reduce any beany flavor and creates a thicker cream.) If you are using tofu in aseptic boxes, just drain the water from the boxes and proceed with the recipe.

2. Combine the tofu, oil, and salt in a food processor, and process about 1 minute until puréed. Use a rubber spatula to clean the sides of the bowl and add the sugar, cocoa, and vanilla. Process 1 to 2 minutes, until the tofu mixture is smooth.

3. Add the melted chocolate and pulse the processor three or four times to incorporate. Process for 1 to 2 minutes, until the mixture is very smooth and creamy. Refrigerate in the processor for 20 minutes. If you used the aseptic boxes of silken tofu, chill the cream for 6 to 24 hours in order for it to become firm.

4. The cream firms when it is chilled, and the degree of firmness will determine the amount of soymilk needed to create the final texture. It should be firm, but similar to a buttercream or similarly textured frosting. If the chilled cream is easy to spread, spoon it into a bowl and begin to assemble the cake. If the chilled cream is too stiff to use, add 6 tablespoons of the soymilk and process 30 to 60 seconds. (If you used 12.3-ounce boxes of silken tofu, you probably won't need to add any soymilk to the cream.) Dip an icing spatula into the cream and test to see if it spreads easily. Add more soymilk, if needed, a tablespoon at a time, processing after each addition.

Carob German Not Chocolate Cake

Yield: one 9-inch two-layer cake (10 to 15 servings)

¾ cup whole wheat pastry flour

¾ cup unbleached white flour

3 tablespoons plus 1 teaspoon carob powder

2 teaspoons baking powder

¼ teaspoon baking soda

½ teaspoon salt

½ teaspoon ground cinnamon

¼ cup canola oil

¾ cup plus 2 tablespoons maple syrup

2 tablespoons barley malt or molasses

¾ cup vanilla soymilk or rice milk

1½ teaspoons vanilla extract

1½ teaspoons apple cider vinegar

Traditional German chocolate cake is made with German's sweet baking chocolate and filled and frosted with a gooey coconut–pecan spread. We can have this spread and eat it too when it is made with a combination of brown rice and maple syrups instead of the white sugar, egg yolks, and heavy cream in traditional recipes. The moist carob cake is good on its own.

1. Position a rack in the middle of the oven and preheat to 350 degrees. Oil two 9-inch round cake pans and line the bottoms with parchment paper cut to fit.

2. Place a wire mesh strainer over a medium bowl. Add the pastry flour, white flour, carob, baking powder, baking soda, salt, and cinnamon to the strainer. Tap the strainer against the palm of your hand to sift the ingredients into the bowl. Stir with a wire whisk to distribute the ingredients.

3. In a separate medium bowl, whisk the oil, maple syrup, barley malt or molasses, soymilk, vanilla, and vinegar until well blended. Pour into the dry mixture and stir with a whisk until the batter is smooth.

4. Divide the batter evenly between the two prepared pans, and smooth the tops with a spatula. Tap the pans lightly on the counter to eliminate air bubbles.

Pecan Coconut Spread
(page 156)

2 tablespoons unsweet-
ened, finely shredded
dried coconut, toasted

5. Bake 25 to 30 minutes, until the tops of the cakes are set and firm, the sides have started to pull away from the pans, and a cake tester inserted in the centers comes out clean or with only a few moist crumbs.

6. Cool the pans on wire racks for 10 minutes. Run a thin knife between the cake and the inside of the pan and invert each layer on a rack. Remove the pans and carefully peel off the parchment paper. Invert the layers again topside up onto a rack. Cool completely.

7. To assemble the cake, spread about half of the spread on top of one layer. Place the other layer on top and cover with the remaining spread. Sprinkle with the remaining coconut.

Pecan Coconut Spread

Yield: 2 cups

2/3 cup brown rice syrup

1/2 cup maple syrup

Dash salt

1/4 teaspoon apple cider vinegar or lemon juice

1/4 cup soymilk, more if needed

2/3 cup smooth cashew butter

2 teaspoons vanilla extract

1/2 teaspoon almond extract

1/2 cup pecans, toasted (see page 23) and cooled

2/3 cup unsweetened shredded dried coconut, toasted (see page 23) and cooled

You will find many uses for this thick, gooey sweet topping. This is another one of those recipes that is hard not to eat directly off a spoon.

1. Place the rice syrup and maple syrup in a small saucepan with a heavy bottom and high sides and bring to a rolling boil. Reduce the heat, add the salt and vinegar, and simmer for 7 minutes. (Hot syrups tend to climb the sides of the pot, so watch carefully.)

2. Slowly whisk the soymilk into the syrup mixture. Simmer 3 more minutes.

3. Remove the saucepan from the heat. Whisk the cashew butter and vanilla and almond extracts into the syrups until well blended. Pour into a heatproof glass or metal bowl, and cool for 5 minutes.

4. Chop the pecans medium-fine. Stir the pecans and coconut into the syrup mixture. Cool to room temperature. The topping should be thick enough to spread. Cover and refrigerate 10 to 15 minutes, to thicken if necessary.

Tip: This filling can be made up to three days ahead and refrigerated in a covered container, or frozen for up to four weeks, but it will need to be softened before using. Set the container in a small saucepan of simmering water and stir vigorously. Add a tablespoon or more of soymilk, if needed, to thin.

Caramel Sauce:

Omit the pecans and coconut. Keep a jar in your refrigerator. It's delicious poured over puddings and frozen desserts, and drizzled on cake (especially the Dark Moist Spice Cake, page 136).

Tart Lemon Spread

Yield: about 2⅓ cups

2 tablespoons agar flakes

1⅓ cups apple juice

½ teaspoon salt

2 pinches turmeric

½ cup maple syrup

½ cup plus 2 table-spoons rice milk

1 tablespoon plus 2 teaspoons arrowroot

⅓ cup fresh lemon juice

1 tablespoon minced lemon zest

¼ teaspoon lemon extract

½ teaspoon vanilla extract

¼ cup rice syrup

The turmeric contributes the bright yellow "eggy" color of this very lemony spread. The flavor is smooth and almost buttery, like lemon curd. Try the spread on toast instead of jam for a nice change.

1. Measure the agar into a medium saucepan. Pour in 1⅓ cups of the apple juice but do not stir or heat. Set aside for 10 minutes or longer to allow the agar to soften. Add the salt and turmeric.

2. Cover the saucepan with a lid and bring to a boil over medium heat. Watch closely because the apple juice has a tendency to boil over. Uncover, reduce the heat to low, and stir to release any bits of agar that may be stuck on the bottom of the saucepan. Cover and simmer for 7 to 10 minutes, stirring a few times.

3. Uncover and check the apple juice in the saucepan, examining a large spoonful for specks of agar. If necessary, cover and simmer longer until the agar has completely dissolved. Add the maple syrup and rice milk to the pot, and simmer for 1 minute.

4. Combine the arrowroot with the remaining 2 tablespoons of rice milk in a small bowl, and stir with a fork to dissolve. Add to the simmering liquid, whisking constantly. Cook over medium heat only until the liquid boils. (If you cook or stir arrowroot-thickened mixtures after they have boiled, they are likely to become thin again.) Immediately remove the saucepan from the heat and add the lemon juice, zest, and lemon and vanilla extracts. Stir gently to mix.

5. Pour the spread into a shallow dish, and refrigerate about 20 minutes until firm. Spoon the spread into a food processor, and process until creamy. Add the rice syrup and process only until well combined. The spread is ready to use, but can be refrigerated in a covered container up to a day ahead.

Cinnamon Walnut Un-Coffeecake

Yield: one tall 9-inch cake (12 or more servings)

Filling

1½ cups walnuts, toasted (see page 23), cooled, and chopped

¼ cup light natural cane sugar or maple sugar

¼ cup dark whole cane sugar

2 teaspoons ground cinnamon

2½ to 3 tablespoons canola oil

This big, moist cinnamon–scented cake was my signature recipe when I baked at Angelica Kitchen, and was a popular choice at the restaurant. It will stay moist and fresh tasting for up to three days.

To make the filling, mix the walnuts, sugar, dark whole cane sugar, and cinnamon in a small bowl. Stir in 2½ tablespoons of the oil. The nuts should be damp, but not wet. Add the remaining oil, if necessary.

1. Position a rack in the middle of the oven and preheat to 350 degrees. Oil a 9 x 3-inch-deep springform pan, and line the bottom with a piece of parchment paper cut to fit.

2. To make the cake, place a wire mesh strainer over a medium bowl. Add the pastry flour, white flour, sugar, cinnamon, baking powder, baking soda, salt, and nutmeg to the strainer. Tap the strainer against the palm of your hand to sift the ingredients into the bowl. Stir with a wire whisk to distribute the ingredients.

Cakes, Frostings, Glazes

Cake

1 cup whole wheat
   pastry flour

1 cup unbleached white
   flour

3 tablespoons light
   natural cane sugar

1½ teaspoons ground
   cinnamon

1 teaspoon baking
   powder

1 teaspoon baking soda

½ teaspoon salt

¼ teaspoon ground
   nutmeg

¼ cup canola oil

¾ cup plus 2
   tablespoons maple
   syrup

¾ cup soymilk or rice
   milk

2 tablespoons vanilla
   extract

1 teaspoon almond
   extract

1 tablespoon apple cider
   vinegar

3. Combine the oil, maple syrup, soymilk, vanilla and almond extracts, and vinegar in a separate medium bowl, and whisk until well blended. Pour into the dry mixture and stir with a whisk until the batter is smooth.

4. Pour half the batter into the prepared cake pan and sprinkle with half the sweet nuts. Pour the remaining batter over the nuts, using a small spatula or thin knife to spread, if necessary. Sprinkle the batter evenly with the remaining nuts.

5. Bake for 40 to 45 minutes or longer, until the cake is golden and firm at the center when touched gently, and a cake tester inserted in the center of the cake comes out clean or with only a few moist crumbs.

6. Place the pan on a wire rack and run a thin knife around the inside of the pan to release the cake. Cool the cake in the pan for 15 minutes, then remove the outside ring of the pan. Cool completely on the rack before cutting.

Big Orange Bundt Cake

Yield: 12 to 16 servings
See photo facing page 145.

1½ cups whole wheat pastry flour

1½ cups unbleached white flour

2 teaspoons baking soda

1 teaspoon salt

½ teaspoon baking powder

1 cup light natural cane sugar

¼ cup dark whole cane sugar

⅔ cup canola oil

1 cup orange juice

1 cup soymilk or rice milk

2 tablespoons apple cider vinegar

2 teaspoons vanilla extract

1 teaspoon orange extract

3 tablespoons finely grated orange zest

This colossal cake elicits oohs and ahs when set out for serving, but the proof is in the tasting and this cake goes to the head of its class. A Bundt pan is a deep pan with a hollow center core, similar to an angel food cake pan, but with fluted sides. The hollow center is necessary to ensure that the large amount of batter bakes through.

1. Position a rack in the middle of the oven and preheat to 350 degrees. Oil a 10- to 12-cup Bundt pan thoroughly.

2. Place a wire mesh strainer over a medium bowl. Add the pastry flour, white flour, baking soda, salt, baking powder, sugar, and dark whole cane sugar to the strainer. Tap the strainer against the palm of your hand to sift the ingredients into the bowl. Stir with a wire whisk to distribute the ingredients.

3. Combine the oil, orange juice, soymilk, vinegar, vanilla and orange extracts, and zest in a separate bowl, and whisk until well combined. Pour into the dry mixture and stir with a whisk until the batter is smooth.

4. Pour the batter evenly into the prepared Bundt pan. The pan will be two-thirds full. (If you have more batter than that, perhaps a cup or so, bake it in one or two 1-cup baking ramekins or custard cups.) Smooth the top of the batter with a small spatula. Rotate the Bundt pan to level the batter, and tap it lightly on the counter to eliminate air bubbles.

5. Bake for 45 to 55 minutes, until the cake is golden and springs back near firm at the center when touched lightly. A tester inserted in a few spots near the center of the cake should come out clean or with only a few moist crumbs.

6. Remove the cake from the oven and cool in the pan on a rack for 15 minutes. Place another wire rack on top of the cake and turn the pan upside down. Shake the pan gently to release the cake. Cool the cake completely before serving.

Big Orange Cranberry Bundt Cake:

Stir 1 cup dried cranberries into the batter after it is mixed.

Variations:

Use two 9-inch round pans that are at least 2 inches deep, or use a 9 x 13 x 2-inch pan to make a sheet cake. Bake for 25 to 35 minutes. Try any of the fillings, frostings, and icings in this book or serve the layers plain. The combination of Soft Orange Tofu Cream (page 58) as a filling with either Ultimate Chocolate Icing (page 147) or Chocolate Ganache (page 133) is absolutely heavenly.

Tip: Drizzle the cake with Soft Orange Tofu Cream (page 58). Stir some dried cranberries into a portion of the orange cream and serve with the cake.

• If the cake sticks to the pan when it is inverted on the rack, wet a kitchen towel in very warm water, wring it out, and place it over the inverted pan for few minutes. Shake the pan gently and the cake should release.

24 Karrot Cake

Yield: one 8-inch two-layer cake (8 to 10 servings)

½ cup raisins

⅓ cup orange juice

1 cup whole wheat
pastry flour

1 cup unbleached white
flour

2 teaspoons baking
powder

2 teaspoons baking soda

1 teaspoon ground
cinnamon

½ teaspoon salt

½ teaspoon ground
mace or nutmeg

½ teaspoon ground
cloves

This is the best carrot cake. It's moist, light, spiced just right, and is a frequently requested wedding cake. Apple cider vinegar has been added to the version of the cake recipe that appeared in my first book, resulting in an even lighter cake.

1. Position a rack in the middle of the oven and preheat to 350 degrees. Oil two 8-inch round cake pans. Line the bottoms with parchment paper cut to fit.

2. Soak the raisins in the orange juice for about 10 minutes, until they are plump. Drain, reserving the juice.

3. Place a wire mesh strainer over a medium bowl. Add the pastry flour, white flour, baking powder, baking soda, cinnamon, salt, mace, and cloves to the strainer. Tap the strainer against the palm of your hand to sift the ingredients into the bowl. Stir with a wire whisk to distribute the ingredients.

4. In a separate medium bowl, whisk the oil, maple syrup, soymilk or rice milk, 2 tablespoons of the reserved orange juice, the vinegar, and vanilla and orange extracts until well blended.

5. Pour into the dry mixture and stir with a whisk until the batter is smooth. Stir the grated carrots and drained raisins into the batter with a rubber spatula.

6. Divide the batter evenly between the two pans and smooth the tops with a spatula.

¼ cup canola oil

1 cup plus 2 tablespoons maple syrup

½ cup vanilla soymilk or rice milk

2 teaspoons apple cider vinegar

½ teaspoon vanilla extract

½ teaspoon orange extract

2 cups peeled, shredded carrots (4 to 6 carrots), firmly packed

Tart Lemon Spread (page 157)

7. Bake for 30 to 35 minutes, until the tops of the cakes are golden, the sides have started to pull away from the pans, and a cake tester inserted in the centers comes out clean or with only a few moist crumbs.

8. Cool the pans on wire racks for 10 minutes. Run a thin knife between the cakes and the inside of the pans. Invert each layer onto a rack. Remove the pans and carefully peel off the parchment paper. Invert the layers again topside up onto racks. Cool completely.

9. To protect the layers from cracking or breaking, slide a cardboard circle under each one. Wrap the layers in plastic wrap, and refrigerate for 1 to 8 hours, until cold, before filling and frosting.

10. To assemble the cake, place one layer on a flat plate and spread with a scant half of the Tart Lemon Spread. Remove the other layer from the cardboard onto the top of the cake and spread with glaze. Push a thin wooden skewer into the center of the cake to keep the top layer from sliding off the slippery glaze. Sprinkle a few shreds of carrot around the outside edge of the cake if you have some left over. Refrigerate about 30 minutes before slicing and remove the skewer.

Amazing Hot Fudge Sundae Cake

Yield: 6 to 8 servings

½ cup whole wheat pastry flour

½ cup unbleached white flour

1¾ cups light natural cane sugar

½ cup unsweetened Dutch-process cocoa

2 teaspoons baking powder

½ teaspoon baking soda

½ teaspoon ground cinnamon

¼ teaspoon salt

¼ cup canola oil

½ cup soymilk or rice milk

2 teaspoons vanilla extract

1¾ cups boiling water

Tip: You won't be able to test whether this cake is done using a cake tester. The top of the cake will look set but still loose when the cake is ready.

Bake this amazing cake during your meal and enjoy a dessert that makes its own sauce in the same baking dish.

1. Position a rack in the middle of the oven and preheat to 350 degrees. Oil a 2-quart baking dish that is 3 inches deep or more. Place the baking dish on a baking sheet to make it easier to move in and out of the oven.

2. Place a wire mesh strainer over a medium bowl. Add the pastry flour, white flour, 1¼ cups of the sugar, ¼ cup of the cocoa, the baking powder, baking soda, cinnamon, and salt to the strainer. Tap the strainer against the palm of your hand to sift the ingredients into the bowl. Stir with a wire whisk to distribute the ingredients.

3. Whisk the oil, soymilk, and vanilla in a separate medium bowl until well blended. Pour into the dry mixture and stir with a whisk until the batter is smooth.

4. Spread the batter into the prepared pan and smooth the top with a spatula. Sift the remaining ½ cup sugar and ¼ cup cocoa into a small bowl and sprinkle evenly over the batter. Pour the boiling water over the batter—this is not a mistake!

5. Bake for about 25 minutes, until the cake is set and the sauce is bubbling up through the top. Cool the cake in the pan for 10 to 15 minutes before serving. Spoon a portion of sauce and cake into each dish.

Cakes, Frostings, Glazes

Chapter 6 . . . Great Good Pies and Tarts

Introducing Great Good Pies and Tarts Naturally

Say goodbye to fear of flaking. The recipes in this chapter include pies baked in pie pans, as well as freeform pies (which are baked directly on a baking sheet) and pressed tart crusts. The pastry dough in this chapter can be used to make savory pies as well.

As a teacher, I've heard veteran and novice bakers alike say they find making pies intimidating, but actually, pies are fast, easy, and made from just a few staple ingredients. And no, you don't need a marble board. Trust me, this is not rocket science, although there are a few "rules" for making outstanding pies, and they are nonnegotiable.

Making pie dough takes a lot less time than reading these notes, but please do read them before you begin. Now repeat after me, "I, (state your name), can make a great piecrust."

Secrets to Making Perfect Flaky Nondairy, Egg-Free Pie Dough

- Think like a pastry chef and get prepared before you start. Read the recipes all the way through and make sure you understand the directions. Put a container of oil in the freezer at least 45 minutes before you plan to mix the dough and make ice water. Plan enough time to allow the dough to rest twice in the refrigerator and for the pie to cool completely before serving. Some fillings need to set for 24 hours.

- Think cold; chill the oil and water, and keep the dough chilled.

- Use a mixture of equal amounts organic whole wheat pastry flour and unbleached white flour. Pastry flour is softer and lower in protein than standard whole wheat (bread) flour, which would make the pastry tough. Piecrusts made with all whole wheat pastry flour taste like cardboard—believe me. Those made with all white flour are unpalatable.

- Use enough water to make the dough, but no more.

- Handle the dough as little as possible using a rubber spatula and plastic wrap, not your hands. (Your hands will conduct heat into the dough.)

- Allow the dough to rest in the refrigerator after it is mixed and again after it is shaped.

- Bake piecrusts in the lower section of a hot oven; crumb crusts should be baked in the middle of the oven.

- Position a rack in the lowest section of the oven and another rack in the middle. The bottom heat will quickly set and brown the crust.

- Preheat the oven to 400 to 425 degrees, depending on the recipe.

- Have the filling prepared and at room temperature.

- Plan ahead; most pies must cool for a few hours to allow the fillings to set and fruit juices to thicken.

Making Blind Baked Piecrusts

Blind baking pastry dough refers to prebaking the piecrust without a filling. Crusts are blind baked when a filling is precooked, not cooked at all, or if a very juicy filling would make a crisp crust difficult to achieve.

• Crumple and flatten a large piece of parchment paper and place it over the crust. Cover the parchment paper with a large piece of aluminum foil (about 16 inches), and fill with dry beans or metal baking beans. The foil will make removing the beans easier.

• Position a rack in the lowest section of the oven and preheat to 400 degrees. Bake for 20 minutes and remove the pan from the oven. Carefully remove the foil and beans, and carefully peel off the parchment paper. Prick the sides and bottom of the crust gently and lightly with a fork. Lower the temperature to 375 degrees. Bake the crust for 5 minutes longer for a partially baked crust or 10 to 12 minutes longer for a fully baked crust. The times are approximate; you need to observe the color of the pastry. If the sides are browning too much, protect them by fitting aluminum foil over them.

Making and Baking Crumb Crusts

• Toast and cool nuts, seeds, oats, and prepare other ingredients as needed.

• Line a baking sheet with a piece of parchment paper. Place a tart pan with a removable bottom on the prepared sheet, and oil the bottom and sides with canola oil. The parchment paper will contain any crumbs that fall when the crust is pressed.

• Cover the crumbs with a piece of plastic wrap to prevent them from sticking to your fingers. Spread in an even layer on the bottom and sides of the pan. Be sure the crumbs are not too thick where the sides and bottom meet. Refrigerate for 15 minutes.

• Preheat the oven to the temperature specified in the recipe, and bake for 15 to 18 minutes, or until the crust is golden brown. Be careful when moving the tart out of the oven; the sides are fragile and easily broken when hot, but will firm as the crust cools. Leave the tart on the baking sheet, and place the sheet on a cooling rack for about 15 minutes. Move the tart pan carefully off the sheet and directly onto the cooling rack, allowing time for the crust to cool completely before filling. To remove a tart ring easily from the bottom, set the cooled tart pan on a wide base (such as a coffee can or mixing bowl). The outer ring should separate from the bottom of the tart. If it sticks, slide a long, thin metal spatula (angled off-set is best) between the base and the ring.

• Crumb crusts can be frozen for up to one month. Wrap in plastic wrap and cover with aluminum foil. Defrost at room temperature for 10 to 15 minutes before baking. Fully baked crusts can be frozen as well.

• To avoid soggy crusts, do not assemble tarts with crumb crusts more than one or two hours before serving.

Fruit and Cream Tarts

This is not a recipe per se; rather it is a method for assembling tarts and tartlets. The yield depends on the size of the tart or tartlet pans.

The fancy fruit tarts and tartlets you see in patisseries are composed of baked crusts filled with creams and covered decoratively with glazed fruit. They look labor-intensive and difficult to make, but in fact the components are made in advance. All the elements you need to design your special version are in this book. And there is more good news: Your tarts will not only taste and look fantastic, they'll also be free of cholesterol, white sugar, and saturated fat.

I have listed some suggestions for complementary combinations and crusts; consult the index for specific recipes. However, feel free to use your favorite components. If you keep some baked crusts in the freezer, you are halfway there. Remember that most creams need to chill for a minimum of four hours, and that twenty-four hours is usually better.

Suggested Amounts

The following amounts are guidelines only; use more or less cream and fruit as you like.

- Use 4 to 5 cups of filling for a 9-inch tart pan
- Use ½ to ⅔ cup of filling for each 4- to 4½-inch tart pan

Suggested Combinations of Fillings and Fruit:

- Soft Orange Tofu Cream (page 58) with Maple Glazed Cranberries (page 141)
- Strawberry Tofu Cream (page 59) with glazed strawberries and other berries
- Ginger Tofu Whip (page 57) with thinly sliced ripe pears tossed with warm orange marmalade
- Tart Lemon Spread (page 157) with blueberries
- Island Coconut Cream Filling and Frosting (page 146) with ripe banana and mango slices

The Crusts

- Use 2 cups of crumbs to make one 9-inch tart pan or four 4- to 4½-inch round tart pans
- Almond Cookie Crust (page 190)
- Oat Sesame Crust (page 76)
- Cornmeal Pignoli Crust (page 192)
- Nondairy Tender Foolproof Flaky Pie Dough (page 172)

Preparation

1. Bake, cool, and store the crust according to the recipe.
2. Make the creams and refrigerate them following the recipe.
3. Prepare the fruit.
4. Warm some jam or melt some chocolate.

Assembly

1. Within two hours of serving, brush the bottom of the prepared crust with warm jam or melted chocolate.
2. Spoon the cream or pudding into the tart or tartlets.
3. Arrange sliced fruit or berries over the cream in any design you like (concentric circles starting at the outside edge, for example, or rows on the entire surface or just half).
4. Refrigerate for up to two hours.

Nondairy Foolproof Flaky Pie Dough

Yield: one 9- to 10-inch single piecrust or tart, or one 11- to 12-inch freeform piecrust, or four to five 4-inch tart crusts

¾ cup whole wheat pastry flour

¾ cup unbleached white flour

½ teaspoon salt

½ teaspoon ground cinnamon

¼ teaspoon baking powder

¼ cup ice-cold canola oil (place a jar in the freezer for 45 minutes)

1 teaspoon apple cider vinegar

3 to 6 tablespoons ice water

Tip: This recipe makes more dough than is needed for a 9- to 10-inch regular or deep-dish pie, tart, or freeform pie, but having an ample amount makes rolling and shaping the dough easier. It is also less likely to stretch when being fitted into the pie or tart pan.

This excellent all–purpose pie dough is suitable for both sweet and savory pies. When properly made, the canola oil–based crust is flaky and a bit firmer than traditional crusts, making it the right choice for berry pies and other pies with juicy fillings. The dough is really quick and easy to prepare, but you need to allow enough time for the oil to chill and the dough to rest twice.

1. Place a wire mesh strainer over a medium bowl. Add the pastry flour, white flour, salt, cinnamon, and baking powder to the strainer. Tap the strainer against the palm of your hand to sift the ingredients into the bowl. Stir with a wire whisk to distribute the ingredients.

2. Slowly drizzle the cold oil over the flour mixture. Using a rubber spatula, toss until the flour is coated with oil. Do not break up the irregular pieces that form. These lumps are equivalent to the solid shortening used in conventional recipes and help to create a flaky crust.

3. Stir the vinegar into 3 tablespoons of the ice water. Add the water gently and slowly to the flour. Add more water a little at a time, if needed, tossing gently until a rough mass holds together. Turn the dough out onto a large piece of plastic wrap. Enclose the dough and use your fingertips to press a round approximately 9 inches wide and 1 inch thick. Chill for 45 minutes or up to 4 hours to allow the gluten to relax.

To roll the dough:

Oil a pie pan or tart pan and place it nearby. Unwrap the dough, and place it between two large pieces of parchment paper. (Do not roll the dough on a floured surface; extra flour will make the dough tough). Use a heavy pin to roll from the center out. Turn the dough 45 degrees and repeat. After one full turn, carefully release the top paper, turn the dough over, release the paper that is now on top, and repeat until the dough is thin (about 1/8 inch thick) and 2 inches bigger than the pan. (The parchment paper will need to be released a few times from both sides of the dough during rolling.) If the dough gets soft or shrinks back during rolling, return it to the refrigerator for 15 minutes.

To fit the dough into a pie or tart pan:

Carefully remove the top piece of parchment paper. Slip your hand underneath the bottom piece, and use it as a carrier to lift and center the dough over the oiled pie pan. Turn the parchment paper over and gently ease the dough into the pie pan. Do not stretch or pull the dough. Trim and save the excess dough, leaving a 1/2-inch overhang.

If the pie will have a crimped (fluted) edge, hold the overhang in and make a decorative edge by pressing the dough, a section at a time, between your thumb and finger. If the dough has softened and is difficult to work with, crimp it just before filling the crust. Cover the surface of the dough with plastic wrap and refrigerate for at least 30 minutes before filling and baking the pie, following the recipe you wish to use.

To fit the dough into a tart pan, place the oiled pan on a parchment-lined baking sheet. Gently center the dough over the pan, taking care not to pull or stretch it, and ease it into the pan, allowing the excess to fall over the sides. Trim the dough with scissors, leaving a 1/2-inch overhang. Press the overhang against the inside of the pan to reinforce the sides of the tart.

To trim the top cleanly, press a rolling pin against the pan edge and roll it across the top. Remove the dough that has been cut off, and clean any dough that may be stuck to the outside of the tart pan. Cover with parchment and plastic wrap, and chill at least 30 minutes before filling and baking the tart, following the recipe you wish to use.

To make a freeform or rustic pie, or galette:

In a freeform or rustic pie or galette, the dough is not fitted into a pie pan; it is baked flat, directly on a baking sheet. It is very easy and the results are very pretty.

Follow the directions for rolling dough for a pie pan, creating a thin (about ⅛-inch thick), 12-inch or larger round or oval shape. I think the rustic, ragged edges are part of the charm of these pies, but the edges can be trimmed with a sharp knife. Move the prepared dough onto a baking sheet, cover with plastic wrap, and refrigerate for 45 minutes or up to 4 hours before assembling and baking the pie, following the recipe you wish to use.

After the dough is rolled out, it can be frozen for up to one week and used to make freeform pies. Wrap the dough tightly in plastic wrap and cover with aluminum foil. Defrost the wrapped dough in the refrigerator. Fill and bake.

Trim the excess dough and save it to make cutouts to bake and place on top of pies and tarts. Cut pieces of dough with cookie cutters, or use a small knife to cut freeform shapes. Sprinkle with sugar and bake on a parchment-lined baking sheet in a 400-degree oven for 8 to 15 minutes. Smaller pieces bake more quickly, so watch carefully to prevent overbrowning. Cool and freeze in an airtight container for up to one month.

Nondairy Tender Foolproof Flaky Pie Dough

Yield: one 10- to 12-inch single pie or tart crust or tart,
or one 11- to 12-inch freeform piecrust, or five 4-inch tart crusts

¾ cup whole wheat pastry flour

¾ cup unbleached white flour

3 tablespoons light natural cane sugar

½ teaspoon salt

½ teaspoon ground cinnamon

¼ teaspoon baking powder

¼ cup ice-cold canola oil (place a jar in the freezer for 45 minutes)

3 tablespoons ice-cold soymilk

3 tablespoons ice water

1 teaspoon vanilla extract

This is my favorite pie dough—period. The addition of a small amount of granulated sweetener, soymilk, and baking powder makes a piecrust so tender, it melts in your mouth. It is a little more difficult to fit into a pie pan, but worth it. If the dough breaks or cracks, just push it back together with very slightly damp fingers and patch with excess dough. You may want to trim the dough before you fit it into the pie pan (use scissors). If the edge is uneven, build it up or cut it down as needed.

1. Place a wire mesh strainer over a medium bowl. Add the pastry flour, white flour, sugar, salt, cinnamon, and baking powder to the strainer. Tap the strainer against the palm of your hand to sift the ingredients into the bowl. Stir with a wire whisk to distribute the ingredients.

2. Slowly drizzle the cold oil over the flour. Using a rubber spatula, toss until the flour is coated with oil. Do not break up the irregular pieces that form. These lumps are equivalent to the solid shortening used in conventional recipes and help to create a flaky crust.

3. Mix the soymilk, ice water, and vanilla. Drizzle 3 tablespoons of this mixture over the flour and oil mixture. Add more liquid, 1 teaspoon at a time as needed, tossing gently until a rough mass holds together. Turn the dough out onto a large piece of plastic wrap. Enclose the dough and use your fingertips to press a round approximately 9 inches wide by 1 inch thick. Chill for 45 minutes or up to 4 hours to allow the gluten to relax.

4. Roll out the dough and fit into a pie pan following the directions for Nondairy Foolproof Flaky Pie Dough (page 170).

Rustic Four-Berry Pie

Yield: one 10- to 12-inch freeform pie (10 to 12 servings)

Crust

1 Nondairy Foolproof Flaky Pie Dough, rolled for a freeform pie and refrigerated (page 169)

Filling

½ cup light natural cane sugar or maple sugar

⅓ cup arrowroot

¼ teaspoon salt

¼ teaspoon ground nutmeg

2 cups fresh raspberries, picked over, rinsed, and patted dry

2 cups fresh blueberries, picked over, rinsed, and patted dry

1 cup fresh blackberries, picked over, rinsed, and patted dry

1 cup fresh strawberries, picked over, rinsed, patted dry, and halved or quartered if large

This is simply the best summer pie. Bursting with thickened berry juices, it looks like it belongs on the cover of a gourmet food magazine.

1. Position a rack in the lowest section of the oven and preheat to 425 degrees. Line a baking sheet with parchment paper.

2. Mix the sugar, arrowroot, salt, and nutmeg in a large bowl. Add the berries and toss gently until coated. Set the berries aside for 10 minutes. The sugar will pull some juice out of the berries.

3. When the oven is hot, remove the prepared dough from the refrigerator. Peel off the top piece of parchment paper, and place the dough on a baking sheet. Spoon the filling on the dough, leaving a 2- to 3-inch border. Fold and pleat the dough up and over the filling (see the photo facing page xx.). Use the parchment paper to help you lift the dough. If the dough tears, patch it with another small piece of dough.

4. Lower the oven temperature to 400 degrees. Bake for 30 to 40 minutes, until the pastry is lightly browned and the filling is bubbling. It's likely the filling will bubble over and the sides may leak, but this is some of the charm of these pies. The filling will thicken as the pie cools.

Tip: Use any combination of berries you like, but the total amount should be 6 cups.

Pear Currant Pandowdy

Yield: one 9-inch pie (6 to 8 servings)

Crust

1 Nondairy Tender Foolproof Flaky Pie Dough (page 172), trimmed to fit the top of a 9-inch pie pan and refrigerated

Filling

6 ripe Bartlett or Comice pears (1½ pounds), peeled, cored, and thinly sliced

1 cup currants

⅓ cup apple or pear juice

¼ cup maple syrup

1 tablespoon fresh lemon juice

2 teaspoons ground cinnamon

¼ teaspoon salt

1 teaspoon vanilla extract

2 tablespoons light natural cane sugar

A pandowdy is a simple, rather plain, old–fashioned dessert that tastes bigger than the sum of its parts. A maple syrup–sweetened fruit filling is covered with a piece of pie dough and baked in the oven. Just before the pandowdy has finished baking, the crust is pushed into the fruit. In New England this is called dowdying.

1. Position a rack in the upper third of the oven and preheat to 400 degrees. Oil a 9-inch pie pan or 2-quart baking dish.

2. Arrange the pears in the pie pan. Scatter the currants on top.

3. Mix the apple juice, maple syrup, lemon juice, 1 teaspoon of the cinnamon, salt, and vanilla, and pour over the pears. Lay the pie dough over the top of the pears. Bake for 35 to 40 minutes, or until the crust is lightly browned. Remove from the oven and cut the dough into squares.

4. Mix the sugar and remaining teaspoon cinnamon, and sprinkle on the crust. Lightly press the crust into the filling and bake for 6 minutes longer. Cool on a rack for 10 to 15 minutes before serving.

Tip: A 9 x 9-inch pan can be substituted for the round pie pan. Cut the dough to fit.

Applesauce Galette

Yield: one 9- to 10-inch freeform galette (8 to 10 servings)

Crust

1 Nondairy Foolproof Flaky Pie Dough (page 169), rolled for a freeform pie and refrigerated

Filling

3 cups unsweetened applesauce, homemade or commercially prepared

1/3 to 1/2 cup light natural cane sugar or dark whole cane sugar

1 tablespoon fresh lemon juice

1/2 teaspoon ground cinnamon

1/4 teaspoon ground nutmeg

1/4 to 1/3 cup all-fruit apricot jam, warmed in a small pot until liquid

When you need a special dessert in a hurry, this is a brilliant choice. Keep some organic applesauce in your pantry and a rolled-out freeform piecrust in your freezer, and your galette will be ready to pop in the oven.

1. To prepare the filling, combine the applesauce, 1/3 cup of the sugar, the lemon juice, cinnamon, and nutmeg in a medium saucepan, and bring to a simmer over medium heat, stirring occasionally, until the applesauce is bubbling and the sugar is dissolved. Taste the applesauce and add more sugar if you prefer a sweeter flavor. Spoon the applesauce into a shallow dish and cool to room temperature.

2. To assemble and bake the tart, position a rack in the lowest section of the oven and another rack in the middle, and preheat to 425 degrees.

3. When the oven is hot, remove the dough from the refrigerator. Peel the top piece of parchment paper off the dough, but keep the dough on the baking sheet. Spread the applesauce on the dough leaving a 2- to 3-inch border. Fold and pleat the dough up and over the applesauce. Use the parchment paper to help you lift the dough.

4. Bake the tart on the lower rack for 40 minutes, until the crust is lightly browned and the apple-sauce is beginning to bubble. Reduce the temperature to 400 degrees and move the tart to the upper rack. Bake for 12 to 15 minutes longer, until the filling is bubbling and the crust is firm and lightly colored.

5. Remove the pie from the oven. Place the baking sheet on a rack. Brush the crust with some of the jam. Cool the tart on the baking sheet for 20 minutes, then slide it, still on the parchment, off the baking sheet onto the rack. Cool to room temperature. The pie tastes best after one or two hours at room temperature. Wrap the tart with plastic wrap and keep at room temperature for two days.

Tip: Use this recipe as a template, and create different fruit sauce–based rustic pies: applesauce and rhubarb or pear and cranberry, for example. Always leave a 2- to 3-inch border of dough to fold up around the filling.

Cranapple Maple Pie

Yield: one 9-inch pie (8 to 10 servings)

Crust

1 Nondairy Foolproof Flaky Pie Dough (page 169), fitted into a 9-inch pie pan and refrigerated

Filling

3 cups fresh or frozen cranberries, picked over and rinsed

3/4 cup maple syrup

1/4 cup orange juice

1/4 teaspoon salt

3 to 4 apples (1 pound)

4 1/2 teaspoons cornstarch

2 tablespoons cool water

This stunning pie is not too rich or sweet, making it a brilliant choice after a big holiday meal.

1. Combine the cranberries, maple syrup, orange juice, and salt in a medium saucepan, and stir to mix.

2. Peel and core the apples. Quarter and chop into small pieces. Add the apples to the cranberry mixture and bring to a boil over medium heat. Lower the heat and simmer for 4 to 5 minutes, until the cranberries begin to pop.

3. In a small bowl, combine the cornstarch with the water, and stir with a fork to dissolve. Add to the simmering fruit mixture, stirring constantly. Cook over medium heat until the liquid boils. Lower the heat and simmer for 1 minute, until the mixture thickens. Remove the saucepan from the heat. Pour the filling into a bowl and cool to room temperature.

4. While the filling cools, position a rack in the lowest section of the oven and another rack in the middle, and preheat to 425 degrees.

5. Spoon the filling evenly into the chilled pie shell. Bake on the lower rack for 35 minutes. Reduce the temperature to 375 degrees. Move the pie to the upper rack and bake 15 minutes longer, until the crust is firm and the filling is bubbling.

6.   Set the pie on a rack and cool to room temperature. Allow the filling to set before serving, about two hours. The pie can be baked a day in advance, wrapped loosely in plastic wrap, and kept at room temperature.

Tip: The cranberry-apple filling makes a wonderful fruit compote. Place the compote in a covered container and refrigerate for up to two days.

Cranpear Maple Pie:

Replace the apples with an equal quantity of firm, ripe pears. Peel, core, and chop the pears into small pieces, and proceed with the recipe.

Sweet Apple Streusel Pie

Yield: one 9-inch pie (8 to 10 servings)

Crust

1 Nondairy Foolproof
Flaky Pie Dough
(page 169), fitted into
a 9-inch pie pan and
refrigerated

Streusel

¾ cup whole wheat
pastry flour

¼ cup dark whole cane
sugar

¼ cup light natural
cane sugar

1½ teaspoons ground
cinnamon

⅛ teaspoon salt

3 to 6 tablespoons
canola oil

Pie bakers and pie eaters seem to have strong opinions about what makes the best apple pie. When I first started my career, I baked in a restaurant in the fall and winter. I made many apple pies daily and started wondering if using a sweet apple would mean less sugar would be needed for the filling. I made a few pies using sweet and readily available Golden Delicious apples and sure enough, I needed very little additional sugar.

1. To make the streusel, combine the flour, dark whole cane sugar, sugar, cinnamon, and salt in a medium bowl, and stir until well mixed.

2. Drizzle 3 tablespoons of the oil over the dry mixture, tossing with a spatula until uneven crumbs form. Add more oil, if needed; the mixture should be damp but not wet.

3. Refrigerate the crumbs in a covered container for 20 minutes or freeze for up to one month.

Filling

5 to 7 large Golden Delicious apples (3 pounds)

3 tablespoons fresh lemon juice

4 tablespoons dark whole cane sugar

1 tablespoon cornstarch

1 teaspoon ground cinnamon

¼ teaspoon ground nutmeg

⅛ teaspoon salt

4. To make the filling, peel, core, and quarter the apples. Cut each quarter into 5 slices. Put the apples in a large bowl and toss with the lemon juice.

5. Combine the dark whole cane sugar, cornstarch, cinnamon, nutmeg, and salt, and mix with a whisk. Add to the apples and stir until the apples are coated.

6. Position a rack in the lowest section of the oven and another rack in the middle. Preheat to 425 degrees.

7. Spoon the filling into the piecrust, mounding the apples slightly higher in the center. Use your hands to pat the apples together tightly. Sprinkle the streusel over the apples and pat it lightly with your hands. Place a round of parchment paper over the streusel and cover with aluminum foil. Bake on the lower rack for 20 minutes.

8. Carefully remove the pie from the oven and set it on a heatproof surface. Lower the oven temperature to 350 degrees. Remove the foil and the parchment paper, and bake on the upper rack for 40 to 45 minutes, until the streusel is golden brown and the filling is bubbling. If the crumbs are getting too brown, cover with the aluminum foil and continue to bake.

9. Set the pie on a rack and cool to room temperature. Allow the pie to set for three hours before serving. The pie can be baked a day in advance, wrapped loosely in plastic wrap, and kept at room temperature.

Pumpkin Pie with Candied Pecans

Yield: one 9-inch pie (8 to 10 servings)

Crust

1 Nondairy Foolproof Flaky Pie Dough (page 169), fitted into a 9-inch pie pan and refrigerated

Filling

1 (14- to 16-ounce) package soft silken tofu (2 cups)

2 cups Spiced Pumpkin Purée (page 55) or 1 (15-ounce) can pumpkin purée

¼ cup dark whole cane sugar

1 teaspoon ground cinnamon

½ teaspoon ground ginger

½ teaspoon ground nutmeg

½ teaspoon ground cloves

¼ teaspoon salt

⅓ cup maple syrup

1 tablespoon canola oil

2 teaspoons vanilla extract

A pumpkin pie with a difference—both dense and creamy with no cream, eggs, or white sugar. The pie needs to chill in the refrigerator for at least five hours, so plan ahead. See the tips following the recipe if you prefer a custard–style pie.

1. Position a rack in the lowest section of the oven and another rack in the middle, and preheat to 375 degrees.

2. To make the filling, drain the water from the tofu but keep it in the container. Cut the tofu into a few pieces and cover with a piece of plastic wrap. Place a heavy object (a box of soymilk or a pot, for example) on the tofu and press for 10 minutes. Drain the tofu and place in a blender or food processor. Process for 3 or 4 minutes until the tofu is puréed.

3. Add the remaining ingredients to the food processor or blender, and purée until smooth. You may need to do this in several batches.

4. Pour the filling into the piecrust. Bake on the lower rack for 20 minutes. Reduce the oven temperature to 350 degrees. Move the pie to the upper rack and bake for 30 to 35 minutes, until the filling has darkened and is shiny. The filling will have cracked and the center will jiggle when the pie is moved; it will firm as it cools. A knife inserted into a crack near the center will come out almost clean.

5. Place the pie on a rack and cool to room temperature. Cover with waxed paper or parchment paper, and refrigerate for 5 to 6 hours.

Candied Pecans

¼ cup maple syrup

2 teaspoons molasses

1½ cups pecan halves

2 tablespoons dark whole
cane sugar

Tips: You can prepare the candied pecans while the pie is baking, and bake them once the oven temperature has been lowered. Alternatively, you can bake and cool the nuts up to two days ahead and keep them at room temperature in a tightly covered jar.

• If you prefer the taste and texture of a custard pie, keep the pie at room temperature for three hours. Cut a small slice as a test to see if the filling is firm enough to serve; let sit for 30 to 60 minutes longer if it's still too soft.

• This may sound like heresy, but I prefer using organic commercial canned pumpkin purée over homemade. It is more consistent in texture, less watery, and more flavorful than homemade pumpkin purée. If you are able to find organic pumpkin pie filling, you can use that as well with no adjustment to the recipe. If you do use fresh pumpkin, choose the smaller, sweeter sugar or cheese pumpkins.

• I often use fresh butternut squash in place of pumpkin.

6. Position a rack in the middle of the oven and preheat to 350 degrees. Line a baking sheet with parchment paper.

7. To make the pecans, mix the maple syrup and molasses in a medium bowl. Add the pecans and toss until well coated. Put the pecans on the prepared sheet in an even layer and toast in the oven for 10 minutes. Remove from the oven and sprinkle with the dark whole cane sugar. Bake 4 minutes and stir. Bake 3 or 4 minutes longer, until the sugar is melted and bubbling and the pecans are nicely browned. Put the baking sheet on a rack and cool the nuts completely. Remove the pie from the refrigerator and bring it to room temperature. Place the nuts decoratively on top of the pie, and serve.

Baking Pumpkin and Squash

To get 2 to 2½ cups of purée, start with a 2-pound pumpkin or squash. Preheat the oven to 400 degrees. Cut the pumpkin in half and discard the stem section and seeds. Place the two halves cut-side down on a baking sheet and bake for about 1 hour, until they are soft. Pierce the skin in a few places to test. Once the pumpkin has cooled, scoop out the flesh into a bowl and purée in a food processor or in batches in a blender. Measure 2 cups for the pie.

Sticky Walnut Tart

Yield: one 9-inch tart (8 to 10 servings)

Crust

1 Nondairy Foolproof Flaky Pie Dough (page 169), fitted into a 9-inch tart pan with a removable bottom, baked unfilled (blind), and cooled

The slight bitterness of the walnuts works beautifully with the sticky sweet syrups.

1. Position a rack in the middle of the oven and preheat to 300 degrees. Line a baking sheet with parchment paper. Place the prepared crust on the baking sheet.

2. To make the filling, pour the maple syrup, rice syrup, molasses, lemon juice, and salt into a large, heavy-bottomed saucepan with high sides, and bring to a boil over medium heat. Lower the heat and simmer for 10 minutes.

3. Remove the saucepan from the heat and whisk in the nut butter, 1 tablespoon at a time. The mixture may look curdled but will become smooth as you whisk. Return the saucepan to the heat and bring the mixture to a simmer over low heat.

4. Combine the arrowroot with the soymilk in a small bowl, and stir with a fork to dissolve. Add to the simmering syrup, whisking constantly. Cook over medium heat, only until the liquid boils. Immediately remove the saucepan from the heat. (If you cook or stir arrowroot-thickened mixtures after they have boiled, they are likely to become thin again.) Add the nuts and vanilla and almond extracts to the saucepan, and stir until the nuts are coated. Pour into a shallow dish and cool to room temperature.

Filling

2¾ cups walnuts, toasted (see page 23), cooled, and coarsely chopped

½ cup plus 2 tablespoons maple syrup

⅓ cup brown rice syrup

2 tablespoons molasses or barley malt

2 teaspoons fresh lemon juice

¼ teaspoon salt

2 tablespoons smooth cashew or almond butter

1 teaspoon arrowroot

⅓ cup soymilk

2 teaspoons vanilla extract

1 teaspoon almond extract

5. Spoon the filling into the prepared crust until three-quarters full, and bake for 20 to 25 minutes, or until the filling is bubbling. The filling may be soft in the center but will firm as it cools.

6. Place the baking sheet on a rack. Cool the tart completely, allowing it to set for two to three hours before serving. Cover the tart with plastic wrap and keep at room temperature for up to two days.

Berry Crisp in a Cookie Crumb Crust (wheat free)

Yield: one 8-inch tart (6 to 8 servings)

Crust

1 cup rolled oats, toasted (see page 23) and cooled

1 cup whole raw almonds, toasted (see page 23) and cooled

½ teaspoon ground cinnamon

¼ teaspoon salt

¼ cup oat, barley, or spelt flour

½ teaspoon baking powder

3 tablespoons unsweetened shredded dried coconut, toasted (see page 23) and cooled

2 tablespoons canola oil

3 tablespoons maple syrup

2 teaspoons vanilla extract

½ teaspoon almond extract

1 to 3 tablespoons fruit juice or water, if needed

Have your pie and eat a crisp too, made in a wheat–free cookie crust. The variation below stems from an email I received from Doug from Brooklyn, who told me that this was one of his favorite recipes and requested a version appropriate for Passover. I was delighted when Doug said my suggestion worked and was delicious.

1. To make the crust, process the oats, almonds, cinnamon, and salt in a blender or food processor until finely ground. Add the flour and baking powder to the food processor, and pulse a few times. Pour the dry mixture into a medium bowl and stir in the coconut.

2. Combine the oil, maple syrup, and vanilla and almond extracts in a small bowl, and whisk until well blended. Pour into the dry mixture and stir until a piece of dough holds together when squeezed. Add the juice, a little at a time, if the dough is too dry. Wrap the dough in a large piece of plastic wrap. Press into a disk and refrigerate for 20 minutes, or up to 24 hours.

3. To bake the crust, allow the dough to come to room temperature. Position a rack in the middle of the oven and preheat to 375 degrees. Line a baking sheet with parchment paper. Place an 8-inch tart pan with a removable bottom on the prepared sheet. Thoroughly oil the sides and bottom of the pan with a brush dipped in canola oil.

4. Press the dough into the tart pan. A piece of plastic wrap placed directly on the dough keeps your hands clean and makes it easier to press evenly on the bottom and up the sides of the pan. Be sure the dough is not thicker where the sides and bottom of the pan meet. When the crust is even, trim any excess dough on the rim with a dull knife. Refrigerate for 15 minutes.

5. Bake on the center rack for 15 to 18 minutes, or until the crust is golden brown. Be careful when moving the tart out of the oven; the sides are fragile and can be easily broken when hot, but will firm as the tart cools. Place the baking sheet on a cooling rack. After 10 minutes, carefully slide the tart off the sheet directly onto the rack and cool completely.

Recipe continues on next page

Berry Crisp in a Cookie Crumb Crust (continued)

Filling

3 cups fresh blueberries, picked over, rinsed, and patted dry

1/3 cup orange juice

6 tablespoons all-fruit berry jam

4 teaspoons arrowroot

1 tablespoon cool water

1 cup sliced strawberries

1 to 1½ cups Good Granola (page 199) or good-quality commercial granola

6. To make the filling, combine the blueberries, orange juice, and 4 tablespoons of the jam in a medium saucepan, and bring to a simmer over medium heat. Simmer for 5 to 7 minutes, stirring a few times until the fruit is very hot and the jam has dissolved.

7. Combine the arrowroot with the water in a small bowl and stir with a fork to dissolve. Add to the simmering fruit mixture, stirring constantly. Cook over medium heat only until the liquid boils. Immediately remove the saucepan from the heat. (If you cook or stir arrowroot-thickened mixtures after they have boiled, they are likely to become thin again.) Pour the filling into a shallow bowl and cool to room temperature. Drain the blueberries, reserving the juice for another use (see tips).

8. To assemble the crisp, spread the remaining 2 tablespoons jam over the baked crust. Spoon the blueberries into the crust and add the sliced strawberries. Sprinkle the granola over the fruit. Gently pull a few strawberries up to peek through the granola.

9. Cover the tart with plastic wrap and refrigerate for 2 to 6 hours. Remove the sides of the pan before serving.

Tips: Refrigerate the reserved berry juice in a covered container for up to three days. Mix more berries into the juice to make a delicious sauce.

• The filling can be made up to one day ahead and refrigerated in a covered container. The crust can be made ahead, wrapped in plastic wrap, covered in aluminum foil, and frozen for up to one month.

Passover Crisp in a Cookie Crumb Crust:

Follow the recipe for Berry Crisp in a Cookie Crumb Crust, replacing the flour in the crust with an equal quantity of matzo cake meal.

Red and Golden Raspberry Lemon Cream Tart in an Almond Cookie Crust

Yield: one 9-inch tart (8 to 10 servings)

Almond Cookie Crust

1 cup whole raw almonds, toasted (see page 23) and cooled

½ cup whole wheat pastry flour

½ cup unbleached white flour

½ teaspoon ground cinnamon

¼ teaspoon salt

¼ teaspoon ground nutmeg

¼ cup canola oil

¼ cup maple syrup

2 teaspoons vanilla extract

1 teaspoon almond extract

This fat–free, tart lemon filling makes a light and gorgeous ending to a summer meal.

1. Position a rack in the middle of the oven and preheat to 350 degrees. Line a baking sheet with parchment paper. Place a 9-inch tart pan with a removable bottom on the prepared sheet. Thoroughly oil the sides and bottom of the pan with a brush dipped in canola oil.

2. To make the crust, grind the almonds to a fine meal in a food processor. Add the pastry flour, white flour, cinnamon, salt, and nutmeg to the processor, and pulse several times. Mix the oil, maple syrup, and vanilla and almond extracts in a small bowl until well blended. With the processor running, pour the liquids through the feed tube in a steady stream. Process only until the mixture holds together. Spoon the crumbs into the prepared tart pan.

3. Cover the crumbs with a piece of plastic wrap to prevent them from sticking to your fingers. Press into an even layer on the bottom and sides of the pan. Be sure the crumbs are not too thick where the sides and bottom meet. Refrigerate for 15 minutes.

4. Bake the crust for 15 to 18 minutes, or until the crust is golden brown. Be careful when moving the crust out of the oven; the sides are fragile and easily broken when hot, but they will firm as the crust cools.

Filling

3 tablespoons agar flakes

1⅓ cups fruit juice–sweetened lemonade

½ cup maple syrup

½ cup plus 2 tablespoons soymilk

⅛ teaspoon salt

Dash turmeric

4 teaspoons arrowroot

½ cup fresh lemon juice

1 tablespoon minced lemon zest

½ teaspoon vanilla extract

1 cup fresh red raspberries

1 cup fresh golden raspberries (see tip)

Mint sprigs for garnish

Half a lemon, thinly sliced, for garnish

Tip: Use 2 cups (1 pint) red raspberries if you cannot find the gold berries. You may also use any other berry or omit them completely and serve the lemon tart plain.

5. Measure the agar into a medium saucepan. Pour in the lemonade, but do not stir or heat. Set aside for 10 minutes or longer to allow the agar to soften. This will help the agar dissolve thoroughly and easily.

6. Cover the saucepan with a lid and bring the liquid to a boil over medium heat. Uncover, reduce the heat to low, and stir to release any bits of agar that may be stuck on the bottom of the saucepan. Cover and simmer for 7 to 10 minutes, stirring several times.

7. Uncover and check the liquid in the saucepan, examining a large spoonful for any specks of agar. If necessary, cover and simmer longer until the agar has completely dissolved. Add the maple syrup, ½ cup of the soymilk, the salt, and turmeric to the agar mixture, and simmer for 2 or 3 minutes.

8. In a small bowl, combine the arrowroot with the remaining 2 tablespoons soymilk, and stir with a fork to dissolve. Add to the simmering lemonade mixture, whisking constantly. Cook over medium heat only until the liquid boils. (If you cook or stir arrowroot-thickened mixtures after they have boiled, they are likely to become thin again.) Immediately remove the saucepan from the heat and stir in the lemon juice, zest, and vanilla. Pour into a bowl, place the bowl on a rack, and cool to room temperature.

9. Pour the filling into the tart shell. Refrigerate for 25 to 35 minutes, until the filling is set.

10. One hour before serving the tart, arrange the raspberries decoratively over the filling in alternating concentric circles or rows.

11. Garnish each slice with a sprig of mint and a thin slice of lemon, and serve.

Glazed Grape Tart in a
Cornmeal Pignoli Crust

Yield: one 9-inch tart (8 to 10 servings)

Tart Crust

½ cup pignoli (pine nuts) plus 3 tablespoons for garnish

1 cup rolled oats, toasted (see page 23) and cooled

½ cup fresh yellow cornmeal

½ teaspoon baking powder

¼ teaspoon salt

2 tablespoons canola oil

3 tablespoons maple syrup

1 to 2 tablespoons fruit juice, if needed

The nutty taste of the cornmeal combines well with the pignoli; these two ingredients are used frequently in Italian cuisine. I based this recipe on a tart I enjoyed in Tuscany. Use fresh, crisp seedless grapes, either all the same variety or a mix of colors.

1. Position a rack in the middle of the oven and preheat to 350 degrees. Place a 9-inch tart pan with a removable bottom on a parchment-lined baking sheet and oil the pan very well, starting with the sides.

2. To make the crust, spread all the pignoli in a small, dry skillet, and stir over low heat for about 1 minute, until they are fragrant but not dark. Cool completely.

3. Process ½ cup of the pignoli, the oats, cornmeal, baking powder, and salt in a blender or food processor until fine. Remove the cover and drizzle the oil over the dry mixture. Pulse a few times until the oil is well incorporated. Add the maple syrup and process until the mixture holds together when pressed between your fingers. Add the juice 1 teaspoon at a time if the dough is too dry.

4. Spoon the mixture into the prepared pan. Cover with a piece of plastic wrap to prevent it from sticking to your fingers. Press into an even layer on the bottom and sides of the pan. Be sure the mixture is not too thick where the sides and bottom meet. Refrigerate for 15 minutes.

5. Bake for 15 to 18 minutes, or until the crust is golden brown. Be careful when moving the crust out of the oven; the sides are fragile and easily broken when hot, but they will firm as the crust cools. Place the sheet pan on a rack and cool the crust to room temperature. Keep in the pan until the tart is served.

Recipe continues on next page

Glazed Grape Tart in a
Cornmeal Pignoli Crust (continued)

Filling

2 pounds seedless grapes (3 to 4 cups)

1½ cups all-fruit apricot jam

3 tablespoons water

2 teaspoons lemon juice

Tips: The tart can be assembled a day ahead. Cover with plastic wrap and refrigerate.

• It is essential to use fresh cornmeal and store it in the freezer or refrigerator to prevent the oils in the germ from becoming rancid. Rancid cornmeal would make the crust taste bitter.

6. To make the filling, wash, dry, stem, and halve the grapes. Put in a medium bowl and set aside.

7. Spread about ¾ cup of the apricot jam on the bottom of the prepared crust.

8. To make the glaze, combine the remaining apricot jam, the water, and lemon juice in a small saucepan, and cook over low heat until the jam is melted. Strain the jam into a small bowl. Save any pieces of fruit for another use. Return the strained jam to the saucepan and simmer over low heat for 1 or 2 minutes until the glaze thickens slightly. Keep the glaze warm.

9. To assemble the tart, pour the glaze over the grapes and toss until well coated. Use a slotted spoon to lift the grapes into the prepared crust. Turn some of the grapes on top cut-side up and some skin-side up. Chill the tart uncovered in the refrigerator for 15 minutes before serving.

10. Carefully remove the sides from the pan, and place the tart on a serving dish. Sprinkle the grapes with the remaining pignolis.

Chapter 7... Great Good Fruit, Beverages, Frozen Desserts, and Confections

Annemarie's Apple Juice
Kuzu Pudding

Yield: 1 serving (about 1 cup)

1 cup apple juice

2 tablespoons kuzu

2 tablespoons cool water

½ teaspoon vanilla extract

Kuzu is thought to soothe the digestive system and relieve stress. This pudding is based on a recipe by Annemarie Colbin, PhD, founder of the Natural Gourmet Institute of Health and Culinary Arts in New York City and author of Food and Healing. *Enjoy this relaxing dessert pudding before bedtime or anytime.*

1. Bring the apple juice to a boil in a small saucepan. Reduce the heat to a simmer.

2. Combine the kuzu and water in a small bowl, and stir with a fork to dissolve. Add to the simmering juice, whisking constantly. Cook over medium heat, until the mixture boils, then cook 1 minute longer, until the juice thickens and clears. Pour into a cup and eat hot or cold.

Annemarie's Apple Juice–Sesame Kuzu Pudding:

Swirl 1 tablespoon tahini (calcium-rich sesame seed paste) into the pudding after it is cooked.

Super Stuffed Baked Apples

4 sweet apples

2 cups apple juice

4 tablespoons raisins

4 tablespoons chopped toasted nuts (see page 23)

½ teaspoon ground cinnamon

¼ teaspoon ground nutmeg

⅓ cup apple butter

Tip: Sprinkle the baked apples with Good Granola (page 199) or a dollop of your favorite tofu whip or nut cream.

Top a warm baked apple with a small scoop of Coconut Sorbet (page 201) and have dessert for breakfast. It's a decadent tasting but perfectly delicious way to begin the day.

1. Position a rack in the middle of the oven and preheat to 350 degrees. Lightly oil an 8 x 8-inch baking dish or other baking dish large enough to hold four apples.

2. Core the apples from the top, stopping 1 inch from the bottom. Peel the top quarter section of each apple. Put the apples in the baking dish, and pour the juice over them.

3. Mix the raisins, nuts, cinnamon, and nutmeg in a small bowl. Spoon the mixture into the apples and sprinkle any leftover filling in the bottom of the baking dish.

4. Cover the apples with a sheet of parchment paper and overwrap with aluminum foil. Bake for 25 minutes. Uncover the dish and baste the apples with the pan juices. Bake 5 to 10 minutes longer, or until the apples are tender but not mushy. The total baking time will depend on the variety of apple.

5. Remove the baking dish from the oven. Brush the warm apples with the apple butter, and stir the remaining apple butter into the pan juices. Serve the apples warm, spooning some of the pan juice over each.

Ultra Creamy Anytime
Oats Sundae

Yield: 1 serving (about ⅔ cup)

⅓ cup rolled oats, toasted (see page 23) and cooled

½ cup soymilk or rice milk

¼ cup plain or vanilla soy yogurt

2 tablespoons chopped nuts (see page 23), or more or less to taste

Chopped fresh fruit, berries, or dried fruit

Maple syrup or brown rice syrup, to taste (optional)

Oats become fantastically creamy after they're soaked for a few hours in soymilk or rice milk. This makes a nutritious, satisfying light meal or hearty snack.

1. Combine the oats and soymilk or rice milk in a small container; cover and refrigerate 8 to 12 hours.

2. Before serving, stir the soy yogurt, chopped nuts, fruit or berries, and maple syrup, if using, into the soaked oats.

Muesli, a mixture of uncooked rolled oats, fruit, seeds, and nuts, was invented by a Swiss physician for his patients. It is easy to digest and packed with iron, calcium, zinc, and other important nutrients.

Good Granola

Yield: about 3 cups

2 cups rolled oats

3 tablespoons dark whole cane sugar

1 cup walnuts, chopped

⅓ cup sunflower seeds

⅓ cup pumpkin seeds

1 teaspoon ground cinnamon

¼ cup frozen unsweetened apple juice concentrate, thawed

1 tablespoon brown rice syrup

1 tablespoon maple syrup

⅓ cup raisins

¼ cup dried cranberries

¼ diced unsweetened dried apricots

Packaged granola is expensive and often too sugary. Make your own and store it in a jar in the refrigerator.

1. Position a rack in the middle of the oven and preheat to 350 degrees. Line a baking sheet with parchment paper.

2. Stir together the oats, dark whole cane sugar, walnuts, sunflower seeds, pumpkin seeds, and cinnamon in a medium bowl.

3. Combine the apple juice concentrate, rice syrup, and maple syrup in a small bowl, and stir until well blended. Pour over the oat mixture and stir until all the ingredients are well coated.

4. Spread the mixture in an even layer on the prepared baking sheet. Bake for 13 to 15 minutes, stirring every 5 minutes until the granola is crisp and golden brown.

5. Put the granola in a medium bowl and add the dried fruit. Stir until well mixed, and set aside to cool. Keep the granola in a covered jar in the refrigerator for up to one week but serve at room temperature.

Chocolate-Coated Frozen Banana Pops

Yield: 8 servings

4 large ripe bananas or 8 small ones

8 wooden Popsicle sticks

8 ounces nondairy semisweet chocolate, finely chopped

½ cup chopped toasted nuts (see page 23)

Frozen bananas taste like ice cream, and this recipe turns them into a sundae on a stick.

1. Line a flat-bottom dish with a piece of waxed paper or plastic wrap.

2. Peel the bananas; cut large bananas in half horizontally. Insert a wooden Popsicle stick into the end of each small banana or the cut end of each piece of large banana. Put the bananas into a container, cover, and freeze for 2 to 8 hours.

3. When you are ready to assemble the frozen pops, put the chocolate in a heatproof bowl set over a saucepan of water. Bring the water to a simmer and stir a few times until the chocolate is melted and smooth. Cool slightly.

4. To assemble the pops, put the nuts in a shallow dish. Hold the stick and dip one banana at a time in the melted chocolate; stir to coat. As you remove each banana, allow the excess chocolate to drip back into the bowl. Roll the bananas in the nuts and return the bananas to the container. Cover and freeze about 2 hours. The bananas can be made ahead and frozen for up to one week in an airtight container.

Coconut Sorbet

1 cup soymilk

1 cup unsweetened
  coconut milk, stirred
  before measuring

1 cup unsweetened
  shredded dried coconut,
  toasted (see page 23)
  and cooled

¾ cup light natural
  cane sugar

2 tablespoons dark whole
  cane sugar

1 teaspoon vanilla extract

Minced zest of 1 small
  lime

This sorbet has a taste reminiscent of toasted coconut ice cream bars.

1. Combine the soymilk, coconut milk, coconut, sugar, and dark whole cane sugar in a large saucepan, and stir to mix. Bring to a simmer over medium heat, stirring occasionally until the sugar has dissolved. Remove the saucepan from the heat, and stir in the vanilla and lime zest.

2. Pour the coconut mixture into a bowl. Cool to room temperature, stirring a few times. Cover and refrigerate 8 to 12 hours to allow the flavors to develop fully.

3. To make the sorbet, pour the mixture through a wire mesh strainer set over a medium bowl. Do not discard the coconut; it will be added back into the sorbet.

4. Freeze in an ice cream maker according to the manufacturer's instructions. When the sorbet is nearly frozen, add the coconut to the ice cream maker.

5. Keep the sorbet in an airtight container in the freezer for up to three days, but allow it to soften slightly at room temperature before serving.

Chocolate Sorbet

Yield: 2½ to 3 cups (3 to 4 servings)

½ cup unsweetened Dutch-process cocoa, sifted

½ cup light natural cane sugar

¼ cup dark whole cane sugar

2 teaspoons cornstarch

2½ cups full-fat vanilla or chocolate soymilk

2 teaspoons vanilla extract

A restaurant in New York City, famous for a dessert it calls "Frozen Hot Chocolate," serves it in a dish with both a spoon and a straw. You can do the same when you serve this delightful, lower fat, non-dairy version.

1. Mix the cocoa, sugar, dark whole cane sugar, and cornstarch in a medium saucepan. Add the soymilk slowly, whisking to mix. Bring the mixture to a boil over medium heat, stirring frequently. Reduce the heat and simmer 2 or 3 minutes, until the sugar has dissolved. Remove from the heat and stir in the vanilla extract.

2. Cool to room temperature and pour into ice cube trays or a shallow container. Cover tightly with plastic wrap and freeze about 6 hours, until solid.

3. Before serving, break the frozen chocolate into chunks. Put the chunks in the bowl of a food processor, and pulse 3 or 4 times until the chocolate is smooth. Return the chocolate to the container and freeze again for 4 to 8 hours. Serve in chilled dishes.

Orange Banana Blueberry Smoothie

1 large peeled frozen banana, broken into pieces

1 cup fresh orange juice

½ cup blueberries, fresh or frozen

½ cup plain or vanilla soy yogurt

1 tablespoon maple syrup or light natural cane sugar

This quick drink is both nutritious and delicious.

Combine all the ingredients in a blender and process until smooth.

Tip: If you want an icier drink and are using fresh berries, add one or two ice cubes to the blender.

Blueberry Peach Walnut Smoothie

2 cups sliced peaches, fresh or frozen

1 cup blueberries, fresh or frozen

1 cup orange juice

½ cup (4 ounces) silken tofu

¼ cup maple syrup, or more to taste

3 tablespoons finely chopped walnuts

1 tablespoon fresh lemon juice

This "meal in a glass" is filled with antioxidants and high in fiber, rich in potassium and omega 3 fatty acids, and loaded with vitamin C.

Process all the ingredients in a blender until smooth. Pour into glasses and enjoy.

New York Eggless Cream

¼ cup Ultimate
 Chocolate Sauce
 (page 63)

1 cup vanilla soymilk or
 rice milk

¼ cup seltzer, club
 soda, or sparkling
 water

*Those of you who remember egg creams probably have strong opin-
ions about the brand of chocolate syrup, the order in which the ingredients are poured into the glass, how to mix, and the Brooklyn
Dodgers, too. I developed this recipe years ago in order to have a
nondairy version of this regional favorite.*

Mix the chocolate sauce and the soymilk in a tall glass with
a long spoon until well combined. Add the seltzer and
enjoy.

Any Nut Butter Puffed Cereal Treats

Yield: one 8 x 8-inch pan (16 to 32 pieces)

½ cup brown rice syrup

2 tablespoons almond butter, smooth or crunchy

1 tablespoon unsweetened Dutch-process cocoa

1½ cups puffed rice cereal

1 cup whole raw almonds, toasted (see page 23) and cooled

1 cup currants

1 cup nondairy chocolate chips

This no–bake, wheat– and maple sugar–free candy is loaded with wholesome ingredients. Vary the nut butter, nuts, fruit, and cereal to create your own version of this fun–to–eat snack.

1. Line an 8 x 8-inch pan with plastic wrap.

2. Pour the rice syrup into a small, heavy-bottomed saucepan with high sides. Bring the syrup to a simmer over low heat. Stir the almond butter and cocoa into the syrup, and simmer for 2 to 3 minutes, stirring frequently with a heatproof spatula until the mixture is smooth.

3. In a large bowl, combine the remaining ingredients, and stir to mix. Slowly pour the warm syrup over the mixture, and stir with a wooden spoon until well coated. Turn the mixture out into the prepared pan.

4. Place a piece of parchment paper directly on the mixture, and press a section at a time to make an even layer. Cover with plastic wrap and refrigerate 30 to 45 minutes, until firm. Cut into squares or bars. Store at room temperature in an airtight container for up to three days.

Tip: As an alternative, shape the mixture into balls and wrap individually.

Caramel Popcorn Treats

Yield: about 6 cups

¼ cup plus 2 tablespoons brown rice syrup

½ teaspoon salt

3 tablespoons barley malt or molasses

1 teaspoon apple cider vinegar

2 tablespoons water

1 tablespoon cashew butter or 2 teaspoons canola oil

1 teaspoon vanilla extract

½ teaspoon almond extract

6 cups air-popped popcorn

½ cup sunflower seeds, toasted (see page 23)

Do you remember looking for the prize in a box of caramel corn? Well, surprise! The real booby prize was the nutritional nightmare in the treat itself: white sugar, corn syrup, molasses, saturated fat, and other poor-quality ingredients. Here is an updated version made with low-calorie, high-fiber popcorn, and featuring brown rice syrup and barley malt instead of refined sugars.

1. Position a rack in the upper third of the oven and preheat to 350 degrees. Line a baking sheet with parchment paper.

2. Combine the rice syrup, salt, barley malt, and vinegar in a heavy-bottomed, medium saucepan with high sides, and bring to a boil over medium heat. Reduce the heat to low, and stir in the water and cashew butter. Uncover and simmer for 4 to 5 minutes, until smooth. Remove from the heat, and add the vanilla and almond extracts.

3. Combine the popcorn and sunflower seeds in a large bowl. Carefully pour the hot syrup into the mixture. Stir with an oiled wooden spoon or rubber spatula until the popcorn and seeds are well coated.

4. Spoon onto the prepared baking sheet. Bake for 6 to 7 minutes, stirring twice until golden brown and almost, but not completely, dry.

5. Cool the sheet on a wire rack. Spoon the popcorn mixture into a container, cover, and keep at room temperature for up to two days.

Bibliography and Reading List

Barnard, Neal. *Eat Right, Live Longer*. New York: Three Rivers Press, 1996.

Bergeron, Ken. *Professional Vegetarian Cooking*. New York: John Wiley & Sons, 1999.

Berley, Peter. *The Modern Vegetarian Kitchen*. New York: Regan Books, 2000.

Bradford, Peter, and Montse Bradford. *Cooking with Sea Vegetables*. Rochester, VT: Healing Arts Press, 1986.

Braker, Flo. *The Simple Art of Perfect Baking*. San Francisco: Chronicle Books, 2004.

Carson, Rachel. *Silent Spring*. Boston: Houghton Mifflin, 1962.

Clark, Robert, ed. *Our Sustainable Table*. San Francisco: North Point Press, 1990.

Coe, Sophie D., and Michael D. Coe. *The True History of Chocolate*. London: Thames and Hudson, 1996.

Colbin, Annemarie. *Food and Healing*. New York: Ballantine Books, 1986.

———. *Food and Our Bones*. New York: Plume Books, 1998.

Corriher, Shirley O. *CookWise*. New York: William Morrow and Company, 1997.

Davis, Gail. *The Complete Guide to Vegetarian Convenience Foods*. Troutdale, OR: NewSage Press, 1999.

Deibel, Karen. *Creating Peaceful Meals*. Columbus, OH: Karen Deibel, 1998.

Eisman, George. *The Most Noble Diet: Food Selection and Ethics*. New York: Diet Ethics, 1994.

Erasmus, Udo, and Jeffrey S. Bland. *Fats and Oils*. Vancouver, British Columbia: Alive Books, 1986.

Gisslen, Wayne. *Professional Baking*. New York: John Wiley & Sons, 1985.

Grogan, Bryanna Clark. *The Almost No Fat Cookbook*. Summertown, TN: Book Publishing Company, 1994.

———. *Nonna's Italian Kitchen*. Summertown, TN: Book Publishing Company, 1998.

Hagler, Louise. *Tofu Cookery*. Summertown, TN: Book Publishing Company, 1991.

Jacobi, Dana. *The Natural Kitchen: Soy!* Rocklin, CA: Prima Publishing, 1996.

Klaper, Michael. *Vegan Nutrition: Pure and Simple*. 4th ed. Summertown, TN: Book Publishing Company, 1999.

Lappé, Frances Moore. *Diet for a Small Planet*. New York: Ballantine Books, 1971.

Madison, Deborah. *Vegetarian Cooking for Everyone*. New York: Broadway Books, 1997.

Melina, Vesanto, Brenda Davis, and Victoria Harrison. *Becoming Vegetarian*. Summertown, TN: Book Publishing Company, 1995.

Ornish, Dean. *Dr. Dean Ornish's Program for Reversing Heart Disease*. New York: Ballantine Books, 1990.

Raymond, Jennifer. *The Peaceful Palate*. Summertown, TN: Book Publishing Company, 1996.

Robbins, John. *Diet for a New America*. Tiburon, CA: H. J. Kramer, 1998.

Root, Waverly. *Food*. New York: Simon & Schuster, 1980.

Sass, Lorna J. *Lorna Sass' Short-Cut Vegetarian*. New York: Morrow Cookbooks, 1997.

———. *Recipes from an Ecological Kitchen*. New York: William Morrow and Company, 1992.

Sax, Richard. *Classic Home Desserts*. New York: Houghton Mifflin, 1994.

Stepaniak, Joanne. *Table for Two*. Summertown, TN: Book Publishing Company, 1996.

Walters, Carole. *Great Pies and Tarts*. New York: Clarkson Potter Publishers, 1998.

Weil, Andrew. *Eight Weeks to Optimum Health*. New York: Alfred A. Knopf, 1997.

Wittenberg, Margaret M. *Good Food: The Comprehensive Food and Nutrition Resource*. Berkeley: Crossing Press, 1995.

Resources for Ingredients and Equipment

Check your local telephone directory and the Internet for sources for ingredients and supplies. Look at listings for natural food stores, Asian markets, and baking supply, cake decorating, and restaurant supply shops. Farmers' markets and food cooperatives offer a good quality, seasonal selection of foods at a reasonable cost. Following is a list of some of the many companies that produce or carry ingredients and equipment for stocking your pantry.

Bob's Red Mill Natural Foods
Stone-ground flours, some organic foods, and much more.
5209 SE International Way
Milwaukie, OR 97222
800-349-2173, 503-654-3215
www.bobsredmill.com

Broadway Panhandler
Bakeware, cookware, knives, and more; good prices and service.
477 Broome Street
New York, NY 10013
866-266-5927
www.broadwaypanhandler.com

Cooking by the Book
The first company to carry the remarkable Microplane aester.
13 Worth Street
New York, NY 10013
212-966-9799
www.cookingbythebook.com

Eden Foods
Organic soymilk, rice milk, liquid sweeteners, oils, apple cider vinegar, agar flakes, agar bars, and kuzu.
701 Tecumseh Road
Clinton, MI 49236
888-441-3336, 888-424-3336
www.edenfoods.com

Equal Exchange
Chocolate and Dutch-process cocoa powder, coffee and teas, all fair trade.
50 United Drive
West Bridgewater, MA 02379
774-776-7400
www.equalexchange.com

Florida Crystals Corporation
Unbleached organic cane sugar, milled (nonorganic) light natural cane sugar.
PO Box 4671
West Palm Beach, FL 33402
877-835-2828
www.floridacrystals.com

Frontier Natural Products Co-op

Nonirradiated spices (bulk available), organic vanilla and other extracts; many other items.
3021 78th Street
Norway, IA 52318
800-669-3275
www.frontiercoop.com

Green & Black's Limited

Organic fair trade chocolate and Dutch-process cocoa powder.
2 Valentine Place
London, England SE1 8QH
Distributed by Belgravia Imports
belgravia@greenandblacks.com
401-683-3323
www.greenandblacks.com

The Hain Celestial Group

Owns many natural food brands, including Walnut Acres and Arrowhead Mills, which makes a wide variety of flours, nut butters, and more.
4600 Sleepytime Drive
Boulder, CO 80301
800-434-4246
www.hain-celestial.com
www.arrowheadmills.com
www.walnutacres.com

Highland Sugarworks

Maple syrup.
Wilson Industrial Park
Websterville, VT 05678
802-479-1747
www.highlandsugarworks.com

King Arthur Flour/The Baker's Catalogue

Organic flours; baking supplies and equipment.
135 Route 5 South
Norwich, VT 05055
800-827-6836, 802-649-3881
www.kingarthurflour.com/shop

Newman's Own Organics

Organic chocolates.
PO Box 2098
Aptos, CA 95001
831-685-2866
www.newmansownorganics.com

New York Cake and Baking Distributor

A dizzying array of supplies for cake making and decorating, chocolate, cocoa powder, and more.
56 West 22 Street
New York, NY 10010
800-942-2539, 212-675-2253
www.nycake.com

nSpired Natural Foods

Their product line includes AH!LASKA organic natural cocoa powder, Sunspire malt-sweetened semisweet chocolate chips and organic dark chocolate, cane juice-sweetened chocolate chips, Sundrops natural chocolate candies, and Tropical Source chocolates.
1850 Fairway Drive
San Leandro, CA 94577
510-346-3860
www.nspiredfoods.com

Rapunzel

Organic chocolate and cocoa powder, Rapadura whole cane sugar (dark whole cane sugar), other organic and fair trade ingredients.
2424 SR-203
Valatie, NY 12184
800-207-2814, 518-392-8620
www.rapunzel.com

Sur La Table

Quality bakeware and supplies, cookware, knives, chocolates, extracts, and much more.
Seattle Design Center
5701 Sixth Avenue South, Suite 486
Seattle, WA 98108
800-243-0852
www.surlatable.com

Suzanne's Specialties

Excellent organic brown rice syrup, barley malt syrup, agave syrup, and more.
A new product, Ricemellow Cream, is the first all-natural vegan marshmallow crème, made with Suzanne's brown rice syrup as the only sweetener.
40 Fulton Street, Unit 7
New Brunswick, NJ 08901
800-762-2135, 732-828-8500
www.suzannes-specialties.com

Vermont Country Naturals

Maple syrup, maple sugar.
PO Box 240
Charlotte, VT 05445
800-528-7021, 802-425-5445

Vitasoy USA

Organic regular and silken tofu, including Nasoya Foods.
One New England Way
Ayer, MA 01432
800-848-2769
www.vitasoy-usa.com
www.nasoya.com

Whole Foods Market

A growing supermarket chain with a great selection and stores in many states.
Many products are organic (including their own "365" brand of tofu, chocolate, and much more). Company policy states that no products with hydrogenated fats are sold in the stores.
550 Bowie Street
Austin, TX 78703
512-477-4455
www.wholefoodsmarket.com

Wholesome Foods

Sucanat (dark dark whole cane sugar), organic and light natural cane sugar.
PO Box 40097
Mobile, AL 36640
251-432-4744
www.wholesomesweeteners.com

Williams-Sonoma

Quality bakeware and supplies, cookware, knives, chocolates, extracts, and much more.
PO Box 7456
San Francisco, CA 94109
877-812-6235
www.williams-sonoma.com

Zabar's

Quality bakeware and supplies, cookware, knives, chocolates, extracts, much more, good prices.
2245 Broadway
New York, NY 10024
800-697-6301, 212-787-2000
www.zabars.com

Organizations and Publications

Center for Science in the Public Interest (CSPI)

Publishers of *Nutrition Action Healthletter*, a great resource.
1875 Connecticut Avenue NW, Suite 300
Washington, DC 20009-5728
202-332-9110
www.cspinet.org

EarthSave International

This organization offers good information from friendly staffers and volunteers. John Robbins, the author of *Diet for a New America,* is the founder.
PO Box 96
New York, NY 10108
800-362-3648
www.earthsave.org

Institute of Culinary Education

Professional programs (mainstream) are offered several times a year as well as recreational programs and intensives.
50 West 23rd Street
New York, NY 10010
212-847-0700
www.iceculinary.com

Natural Gourmet Institute for Health and Culinary Arts

A 600-hour professional chef training course is offered several times a year. Full and part-time classes are available. The associated Natural Gourmet Institute for Food and Health offers a variety of cooking, baking, and lecture classes to the public. Friday night dinners prepared by students in the professional program sell out quickly; reservations are suggested.
48 West 21st Street
New York, NY 10010
212-645-5170
www.naturalgourmetschool.com

North American Vegetarian Society (NAVS)

NAVS is a great resource for books and magazines, and a subscription to its magazine, *Vegetarian Voice*, is free with membership. The annual Summerfest (often in July) is fun and informative. Delicious vegan meals are served, supervised by Culinary Olympics gold medal winner and author Ken Bergeron.
PO Box 72
Dolgeville, NY 13329
518-568-7970
www.navs-online.org

Physicians Committee for Responsible Medicine (PCRM)

A nonprofit organization made up of over 4,000 physicians and laypeople who believe that diet and lifestyle affect health. PCRM focuses on preventative medicine and promotes vegan diet, ethical research methods, and compassionate medical policy.
PO Box 6322
Washington, DC 20015
202-686-2210
www.pcrm.org

Pure Food Campaign

This group supports reforming school food programs and an international ban on genetically engineered foods.
800-253-0681
www.organicconsumers.org

Vegetarian Resource Group (VRG)

VRG promotes vegan and vegetarian nutrition. Their magazine, *Vegetarian Journal*, is published bimonthly and is included with membership.
PO Box 1463
Baltimore, MD 21203
410-366-8343
www.vrg.org

Numerous magazines, such as *Natural Health*, *Organic Style*, *Vegetarian Times*, and *VegNews* are available on newsstands and by subscription.

Common Weights and Measures

3 teaspoons	1 tablespoon	$\frac{1}{2}$ ounce
4 tablespoons	$\frac{1}{4}$ cup	2 ounces
5 tablespoons plus 1 teaspoon	$\frac{1}{3}$ cup	$2\frac{1}{4}$ ounces
8 tablespoons	$\frac{1}{2}$ cup	4 ounces
$\frac{3}{4}$ cup plus 2 tablespoons	$\frac{7}{8}$ cup	7 ounces
16 tablespoons	1 cup	8 ounces
2 cups	1 pint	16 ounces
4 cups	1 quart	32 ounces
1 pound apples	3 cups peeled, cored, sliced	
1 dry pint raspberries	$1\frac{1}{2}$ cups (approximate measure)	
1 dry pint strawberries	2 cups (approximate measure)	
1 medium lemon	2 to 3 tablespoons juice	2 to 3 tablespoons zest
1 pound raisins	$2\frac{1}{2}$ cups	
1 pound whole almonds	$3\frac{1}{4}$ cups	
$\frac{1}{2}$ cup chocolate chips		3 ounces

Page references in *italic* denote where a recipe is also used as an ingredient.

Index

Page references in *italic* denote where a recipe is also used as an ingredient.

Page references in *italic* denote where a recipe is also used as an ingredient.

Page references in *italic* denote where a recipe is also used as an ingredient.

Page references in *italic* denote where a recipe is also used as an ingredient.